STOP ROMA
COLLEGE, LI

Ultimate guide for winning in your teenage & 20s
SAMYAK PATTNAIK

BLUEROSE PUBLISHERS
India | U.K.

Copyright © Samyak Pattnaik 2024

All rights reserved by author. No part of this publication may be reproduced, stored in a retrieval system or transmitted in any form or by any means, electronic, mechanical, photocopying, recording or otherwise, without the prior permission of the author. Although every precaution has been taken to verify the accuracy of the information contained herein, the publisher assumes no responsibility for any errors or omissions. No liability is assumed for damages that may result from the use of information contained within.

BlueRose Publishers takes no responsibility for any damages, losses, or liabilities that may arise from the use or misuse of the information, products, or services provided in this publication.

For permissions requests or inquiries regarding this publication,
please contact:

BLUEROSE PUBLISHERS
www.BlueRoseONE.com
info@bluerosepublishers.com
+91 8882 898 898
+4407342408967

ISBN: 978-93-6783-148-9

Cover Design: Sadhna Kumari
Typesetting: Pooja Sharma

First Edition: November 2024

To my Parents and sister for always supporting me in whatever I desired to do, Hope I can soon repay them by making them proud.

To every one who has at any point been a part of my life and stood with me as a friend, mentor or Partner But no more.

Embrace the journey of learning, for in every challenge lies an opportunity to grow. Your time in college is a canvas—paint it with curiosity, passion, and resilience. Seize the knowledge, forge connections. Your education is not just about acquiring a degree; it's about sculpting the extraordinary person you are meant to become. Embrace the challenges, celebrate the victories The canvas is yours; create a masterpiece." -

HOW TO GET THE MOST OUT OF THIS BOOK

Before you start reading there are certain points that you must follow and religiously follow while interacting with this guide.

- **Stay Open-Minded**: Approach the book with an open mind, acknowledging that everyone's college experience is unique. Be prepared to encounter perspectives that may differ from your own.

- **Reflect on Personal Experiences**: As you read, reflect on your own experiences or expectations about college life. Consider how the insights shared in the book align with or challenge your preconceptions.

- **Take Notes**: Jot down key points, quotes, or passages that resonate with you. This can help reinforce your understanding and serve as valuable references for later reflection.

- **Engage with the Material**: Actively engage with the content by asking yourself questions, making connections to your own life, and considering how the information presented relates to broader societal trends or issues.

- **Consider Multiple Perspectives**: Recognise that the book may present a variety of perspectives on college life, including those of students, professors, administrators, and researchers. Try to understand the motivations and perspectives of each voice.

- **Discuss with Others**: If possible, engage in discussions about the book with classmates, friends, or mentors. Sharing perspectives and insights can deepen your understanding and offer new insights that you may not have considered on your own.

- **Apply Practical Advice**: Pay attention to any practical advice or tips offered in the book for succeeding in college. Consider implementing strategies that resonate with you into your own academic, social, and personal routines.

- **Take Breaks**: Don't feel pressured to read the entire book in one sitting. Take breaks when needed to avoid burnout and give yourself time to process the information.

- **Action Plan**: Consider creating an action plan based on the insights gained from the book. Identify specific goals or changes you want to make in your college life and outline steps to achieve them.

CONTENTS

CHAPTER 1: THE COLLEGE ILLUSION 2

CHAPTER 2: TOXIC FRIENDS CULTURE 11

CHAPTER 3: DILEMMA OF THINKING EVERYONE HAS FIGURED OUT EVERYTHING. THE "COLLEGE ILLUSION" 26

CHAPTER 4: CAMPUS ZEN: MASTERING MENTAL HEALTH IN COLLEGE 39

CHAPTER 5: RED FLAG GREEN FLAG: LOVE UNFILTERED 58

CHAPTER 6: USING FREEDOM, THE RIGHT WAY 98

CHAPTER 7: WORDPLAY: MASTERING THE CHAT GAME THE FILTER COFFEE TECHNIQUE 110

WHY YOU SHOULD STOP ROMANTICISING COLLEGE LIFE

Chapter 1
THE COLLEGE ILLUSION

Now let's start with what this book revolves around "the so-called romantic collage life". Here romantic doesn't mean your love live, or finding love in collage and its definitely not going to one of those Chetan Bhagat novels either. Here the "so called romantic collage life" refers to the romanticizing of one's collage life, the expectations they carry before journeying into collage or to put simply dreaming of the ideal collage life.

Movies like Student of the year, Main Hoon Na, Jaane Tu Ya Jaane Na, 2 states have set some bar, right? Like this perfect collage life where you find the best of friends, fall in love, hangout with your buddies, plan trips to Goa or Manali

And the entire collage seems to be your personal spotlight. Well sorry to break it to you that's not how it works in reality.

Many movies, books, and social media make college seem like a perfect, carefree time full of freedom and happiness. This idealized view can create unrealistic expectations because it doesn't show the difficult challenges students actually experience. It's important to understand that college is not always as perfect as it's portrayed and to have a more realistic perspective on the ups and downs of this important time in life.

Unrealistic expectations: Romanticizing college life can create unrealistic expectations about what the experience will be like. This may lead to disappointment and dissatisfaction when reality doesn't align with the idealized image.

Pressure to conform: When college life is romanticized, there may be pressure on students to conform to a particular image or lifestyle. This can result in students feeling the need to live up to unrealistic standards, leading to stress and anxiety.

Neglect of mental health: The emphasis on the glamorous aspects of college life may downplay the challenges and stress that students often face. This can discourage individuals from seeking help for mental health issues, as they may feel that they are the only ones struggling.

Overemphasis on social aspects: While socializing and building connections are important aspects of college life, romanticizing the social scene may overshadow the importance of academics, personal development, and career preparation. This can lead to a lack of focus on educational goals.

Life After College: The focus on the college years may distract from the importance of preparing for life after graduation. Emphasizing the broader skills gained during education, rather than just the social aspects, can better equip students for the challenges they'll face in the real world.

According to the National Health Assessment, around 80 percent of college students reported feeling overwhelmed. Moreover, 40 percent of college students reported that it was difficult for them to function. Burnout leads to decreased physical and mental health levels, often leading to anxiety and physical pain.

The remedy to balancing your expectations lies in finding that sweet spot where you don't lose the excitement of starting your college journey, but at the same time, you don't let unrealistic dreams weigh you down. It is easy to dive into college life with the desire to do it all—excel academically, make tons of friends, join every club, stay fit, and somehow still have time to chill. While that enthusiasm is essential to making the most of your experience, it can also become overwhelming if you set expectations that are too high or impractical.

College however fails to acknowledge the fact that our difference and unique perks and qualities are our strengths rather portrays them as being different than the stereotypical *"popular college persona"*

1. The Social Butterfly

Meet the Social Butterfly. This is the person who seems to be everywhere—every party, every college fest, every random house party. You wonder if they secretly have a time machine or just zero assignments. They make it seem like the key to a successful college life is being constantly surrounded by a sea of people. While it's great to be social, not everyone wants to party-hop every weekend. Some of us prefer a chill evening with Netflix and, of course, *Maggi*. The problem is college makes you feel like you're missing out if you're not out there "socializing" all the time. But hey, sometimes peace is found in quiet, not in the middle of a crowded DJ night.

2. The Superficials

Now, here come the Superficials. These are the ones who've mastered the art of the Instagram filter, and their life seems like a perfectly curated highlight reel. They're all about appearance, social media clout, and maintaining a "cool" image—because what's more important than impressing people you barely know, right?

The truth is, a lot of them end up neglecting their real personalities just to fit in. It's like pretending you're a *coffee person* when you actually crave some authentic *masala chai*. But let's be honest—none of us are going to remember how "cool" someone looked at the college fest in ten years. What will matter is whether you found your true self or just played dress-up for four years.

3. The Athletic

Ah, the athletes. College life really likes to hype up the idea that being good at sports makes you popular, like you'll somehow unlock a VIP pass in the minds of every guy or girl in the entire college.

But this whole "athletes are automatically cool" thing? Yeah, not really. Whether you're on the cricket team or just casually good at it doesn't define your college experience. And for those of us whose idea of a workout is running to class when we're late, it's totally okay. You don't need to be a sports star to leave a mark on campus.

4. Confidence Overdrive

We all know this one. The *Confidence Overdrive* student walks around like they own the place, and maybe even the entire university. They're the ones who answer every question in class (even the ones nobody asked), and they talk like they've got life figured out. They radiate confidence, but sometimes, it comes off as arrogance.

While it's good to be confident, there is a thin line between self-assurance and being *that person* who dismisses everyone else's opinions. We have all met someone who can't handle a differing viewpoint. Confidence is great, but real confidence means being open to learning from others—not thinking you're always right. Nobody likes a one-person show, after all.

Embracing Your True Self in College

The problem with these stereotypes is that they create a weird pressure to fit into roles that don't actually make sense. College is supposed to be about discovering who you are, but instead, it feels like you have to audition for a role in a movie that no one's watching. If you're not the Social Butterfly, people assume you're missing out. If you're not rocking the Superficial's Insta-ready look, you feel like you're falling behind. And if you're not dominating on the sports field or walking around with *over-the-top confidence*, you start questioning if you're doing college "right."

But here is the thing—there *is no* "right" way to do college. If you're quiet, that's your strength. If you'd rather spend time with a few close friends than at a massive party, more power to you. If your idea of fun is geeking out over a good book or mastering a coding challenge instead of going to the gym every day, embrace it.

College should be about being unapologetically *you*. Whether that means you're the friend who's always ready for a *midnight chai* run or the one who keeps the squad grounded when everyone else is spiraling over exams, your uniqueness is your superpower. It is easy to feel like you need to change to fit into some predefined box, but that's like putting *ghee* in your chai—it's just not necessary.

The best thing you can do is embrace who you are and find people who appreciate that. Don't feel pressured to attend every party, fake confidence, or become someone else to impress people who probably don't matter in the long run. You're not a "lesser" college student because you don't fit into the stereotype. In fact, the real magic of college comes from embracing all the quirks, quiet moments, and chaotic ones too.

At the end of the day, college is a journey, not a performance. And trust me, nobody's judging your script as harshly as you think. So, drop the act, live the reality, and create your own version of what being a college student means

<u>Well, then whose fault is it that such standards have become the mainstay? College itself?</u>

College websites and brochures often paint an idealized picture of student life, enticing prospective students with the promise of a transformative experience. While this approach aims to attract more admissions and enhance the college's brand value, it tends to overlook the profound impact it has on shaping the mindset of both students and society.

The responsibility for perpetuating these standards cannot be solely placed on colleges; rather, it is a complex interplay involving societal and cultural influences. The depiction of an aspirational college culture has deep historical roots and undergoes generational transitions. The "need to be liked" theory comes into play here, where students are driven by a fundamental human desire for acceptance and approval. However, this pursuit of universal approval has given rise to a toxic culture that places undue importance on specific attributes and qualities, often sidelining individuals whose characteristics do not align with the narrowly defined ideals of popularity.

Human beings, as social animals, naturally crave a sense of belonging and affirmation. However, this innate drive has, over time, transformed into a culture that elevates certain traits to a superior status. This, unfortunately, results in the exclusion and neglect of individuals who do not conform to the narrow parameters of the so-called "popular" categories. Recognizing and challenging these ingrained norms is crucial for fostering a more inclusive and diverse college environment that celebrates the uniqueness of each individual rather than perpetuating harmful stereotypes.

Social media's *role in creating this so called "best four years of your life." Image*

Social media can play a significant role in creating and perpetuating fake expectations related to college life. Here are some ways in which this phenomenon occurs:

Crafting a curated image: Individuals often share only the high points of their college experiences on social media, showcasing the most exciting and positive aspects while omitting challenges and mundane moments. This selective sharing can distort the perception of college life, leading others to compare their experiences and develop unrealistic expectations.

Pressure and comparison among peers: Witnessing peers engaging in various activities or achieving specific milestones on social media can create a sense of pressure to conform or compete. Students may feel obligated to meet certain expectations set by their peers, even if these expectations don't align with their own interests, abilities, or priorities.

Influencers shaping perceptions: Social media influencers, often sponsored by brands, may portray an exaggerated or glamorous version of college life. Their content, featuring luxurious lifestyles, expensive belongings, or extravagant events, can set unrealistic standards for the average college student.

Emphasizing accomplishments: Individuals may frequently share their academic achievements, extracurricular successes, or social triumphs on social media. While it's valid to celebrate these accomplishments, the continuous exposure to such content may lead others to believe that everyone is excelling in every aspect of their college experience, fostering unrealistic expectations.

Validation through peers: Social media platforms thrive on the exchange of likes, comments, and shares. Students may seek validation through these online interactions, contributing to a culture where the pursuit of external validation becomes more significant than personal growth and genuine experiences.

My personal college experience - The reason behind writing this so-called guide into not Romanizing college life

First let's start with the obvious mistakes I made:

Choosing my college, well my choice of college was solely based on following the popular opinion, I followed what majority of my friends and peers were doing and that might just be the biggest mistake. Currently in my final year I reflect back and I think that choosing a collage should be based on your interests, personality and career just choosing a college that the popular kids are going to won't benefit yourself and that brings me to the next chapter, Now you have followed the popular opinion and joined an college, the need for approval and the need to be liked pills up as you want to be popular so what do you do you try to fit in, try to be cool create a superficial personality for others surpassing your individuality and in turn harming your own mental health. Well, I did the same I tried to fit in instead of being myself and that definitely took a Toll on my mental health. For the first year of my undergrad went in trying to be someone I'm not, hanging out with the "popular gang", letting validation by others decide my mood and trying to fit in the bubble.

It took be an absolute one year and yes for some it takes them the whole 3 or 4 years of undergrad to get out of the toxic culture and some don't even make out. I was lucky to have some "real friends" in the second year that gave me that motivation to get away from what I was trying to be and what I really wanted. Fast forward to my second year and now I was enthusiastic I stared with joining clubs that actually called out to my interests not what the popular opinions was, I hung out the people because I actually liked spending time with them and engaging in meaningful conversations rather than trying to fit into a group of people for the sake of so-called popularity. For the first time I was finally Happy.

I woke up every day excited to attend collage

Chapter 2
TOXIC FRIENDS CULTURE

College is a place where you meet diverse people, from different backgrounds, experiences and perspectives and that if you follow can college website that is used as a huge selling point of the whole college experience but the other perspective isn't always discussed. Yes, you meet a lot of diverse people and gain perspective, but you also come along certain people who become your friends who can have a drastic negative effect on you. These friends may exhibit toxic behaviors or attitudes that slowly erode your self-esteem, sow seeds of doubt, or lead you down paths that are detrimental to your well-being. Despite the initial camaraderie, their influence can leave you feeling drained, anxious, or even questioning your own values and beliefs. Recognizing these toxic relationships can be challenging, especially when they're masked by the guise of friendship.

During my early days of college, I made the mistake of trying too hard to fit in. This led me to seek out friendships and groups that promised popularity and validation. I longed to be part of the "cool crowd," reeling in the attention as I walked down the corridors, attending wild parties without limits, and becoming the person everyone knew on campus. At first, it seemed exhilarating, but the mental toll that followed was overwhelming.

When you pursue friendships in this manner, you inevitably encounter numerous toxic individuals.

Now, let's delve into why this happens.?

Before that, let's properly analyze

"The concept of friendship."

Friendship is a profound and mutually supportive bond between two or more individuals characterized by trust, empathy, understanding, and shared interests or experiences. It entails companionship, loyalty, and a readiness to provide emotional support, encouragement, and assistance to one another through both joyful and challenging times.

Now, onto the reason. When we forge friendships through such avenues, they often prove fleeting because of selfish or ulterior motives, such as my desire for popularity. We fail to establish foundations of understanding, trust, or mutual empathy. Instead, we remain ignorant of the true selves of those around us, as everyone engages in pretense to fit in.

Friendships built on superficial motives like the desire for popularity or validation lack the depth and authenticity necessary for long-term support and growth. Rather than fostering trust and empathy, these relationships prioritize surface-level interactions and maintaining a specific image or status within a social group.

Additionally, when individuals prioritize fitting in over being true to themselves, they may ignore red flags or warning signs of toxic behavior in others. They might overlook or rationalize negative traits or actions in their friends to preserve the illusion of acceptance and belonging.

Moreover, the dynamics of such friendships can intensify feelings of insecurity and inadequacy. Constantly seeking validation from others and basing one's self-worth on external factors, such as popularity or social status, can create a cycle of dependence on toxic relationships for validation and acceptance.

In essence, the pursuit of popularity or fitting in can lead individuals to form shallow, transient connections with others, where the focus is on outward appearances rather than genuine connection and support. This can ultimately leave individuals vulnerable to the negative influences of toxic friendships and hinder their personal growth and well-being in the long run.

The Ripple Effects of Toxicity

Toxic friendships aren't just Inconvenient —they can seriously mess up your schoolwork and mental wellbeing. Always having to make up for your friend's short comings can stress you out, make you anxious, and make you resentful. It feels really unfair and can make you feel like giving up. It doesn't stop there. Those bad habits can spread. If your friend is always procrastinating, being irresponsible, or lying, you might start doing the same. Before you know it, your grades start slipping, and you're not as committed to your schoolwork. What started as helping out a friend can end up ruining your own academic success.

The Road to Detoxification

Recognizing when things are bad is the first step to making them better. Next, you need to decide what's okay and what's not okay for you. Help out others, but don't let it harm your studies. Work together, but don't let anyone take advantage of you. Most importantly, talk about how you feel. Tell them if something bothers you and explain how it affects you. If they don't listen, maybe it's time to think about whether the friendship is worth it.

College is a time to learn and grow, both in classes and as a person. It's when you learn to take care of yourself, be responsible, and understand how important it is to respect each other. Sometimes, the hardest times teach us the most important lessons. Even if a friendship is difficult, it can show us things about ourselves that we didn't know before.

Mending toxic friendships

Not all toxic friends are necessarily bad people. Some might not realize how their actions affect others, while others might enjoy putting others down to feel better about themselves. Regardless, it's important to set clear boundaries with these friends as a first step. This could involve limiting the time you spend with them, having a serious talk about changing the dynamic of the friendship, or even distancing yourself from them altogether.

it's easy to overlook toxic friendships to avoid drama. However, the close-knit college environment might make it harder to break away from people who negatively impact your mental and emotional well-being. Additionally, it can be tough to end an unhealthy friendship when it comes with perks like invites to parties, connections for internships or maintaining a certain status quo

Ultimately, each student needs to ask themselves whether it's more important to keep a toxic friend around or to stick to their values and surround themselves with supportive friends. While all relationships have their ups and downs, if a friendship consistently leaves you feeling drained, it's likely toxic. Take some time to reflect on whether the stress and drama of the relationship are worth it.

Evaluate your friendships and relationships and consider whether any need to be "cleaned out."

What's what?

Now trying to Figure out toxic traits might not be that simple or straight forward majority of times. Yes, actions are the clear indicators of whether someone is exhibiting such behavior, but Certain phrases, words or conversations topics might seem harmless or inoffensive but are meant to target your subconscious and induce the ripple effect of toxicity which we discussed. Therefore, it is vital that we have a rough understanding of how such phrases or topics look like so that we are mentally ready to Tackle them.

Below are a few such examples

1. 'You're just too sensitive'

When friends claim "you're too sensitive," they suggest your emotions aren't legitimate and imply there's a flaw in you for feeling them. However, sharing feelings is a normal aspect of friendship, and being labeled as overly sensitive could hint at your friend's lack of empathy.

2. 'Can't you take a joke?'

In healthy friendships, being responsive means friends make an effort to understand your feelings and adapt their actions accordingly when you express hurt. However, in toxic friendships, instead of showing understanding, they may use phrases like "Can't you take a joke?" to deflect from hurtful remarks and evade responsibility.

3. 'You're lucky to have a friend like me.'

In strong friendships, equality is key. Both parties are equally committed, and neither sees themselves as superior to the other. If your friend frequently claims superiority or implies you should feel lucky to have them around, it could indicate an unequal relationship where your worth isn't recognized.

4. 'I miss the old you.'

Friends should accept you as you are, regardless of whether your beliefs align with theirs, and support your personal development. If your friend shows unease with positive changes or, worse, diminishes your growth, it might indicate that either you've moved beyond the friendship or your friend isn't genuinely concerned about your well-being.

5. 'You owe me one.'

Reciprocity holds significance in friendships, but if a friend anticipates repayment for every favor, it could suggest they view the relationship as transactional. As you grow closer to someone, you integrate them into your identity, meaning their pain affects you and their joy brings you happiness. This is why true friends feel at ease being generous.

6. 'What's the need of having a party, it isn't such a big deal.'

Having a friend who belittles your achievements or attempts to outshine your success (for example, saying, "Well, it wasn't that difficult of a task anyways") undermines your confidence and happiness. In positive friendships, friends enhance your happiness by enthusiastically congratulating you or celebrating with you.

7. 'I'm sorry you feel that way.'

Genuine reconciliation entails both parties acknowledging the harm they've inflicted. When a friend apologizes solely because of how you feel, it suggests they're attributing the issue to your emotions rather than their actions. If attempts to address your concerns or establish boundaries are met with dismissive responses like this, your friend isn't accepting responsibility for their impact on you.

8. '...' Closure isn't overrated

When a friendship ends, it can evoke a type of grief known as "disenfranchised grief, "This feeling becomes even more intense when you're left wondering why your friend is withdrawing. Being ghosted can cause feelings of hurt, sadness, and diminished self-esteem. Even if someone wants to terminate a friendship, they should demonstrate respect by communicating their intentions clearly and provide a proper closure to the other person.

Now let's come to a very interesting part of the chapter. So far, we discussed how toxicity develops, detecting toxic people, how friendship dynamics changes and how to manage them effectively. Now let's look at how we can manage and mend ourselves into healthy and positive friendships in college.

FINDING THE RIGHT PEOPLE EARLY ON

Like we discussed we meet and interact with diverse people in a collage environment and making sure that you enter into positive friendships and companionships early on will play a vital role in shaping your academics, mood states and overall development.

* Making friends through superficial and keeping selfish motives in mind is a big no.

Keep in mind what you value in a friendship -

This will greatly differ from person to person but there are certain characteristics that everyone values such as reliability, loyalty and trust and so on. When you begin college, you have a great opportunity to interact with people, so initiate conversation with your batch mates, sometimes short conversations give you a brief idea about how the person's thought process is or what morals they value. As our morals are closely related to our personality and subconscious mind isn't often what makes up a person and isn't likely to fluctuate. Therefore, building a bond over shared Morals builds a strong base or foundation for friendships and enables constructive communication even when time gets tough.

Your interests and goals

Shared interests and goals are also a very great starting point unto which a bond can be built. When two people have the same interest and goals, they tend to be determined to achieve them and this can build comrades and a pattern of mutual support. The healthy competition to keep up with you friend will keep you motivated and on track. Moreover, they can engage in meaningful discussions, share experiences, and offer each other valuable insights and advice. This mutual understanding creates a solid foundation for trust and cooperation, strengthening the bond between them. Overall, shared interests and goals provide a strong framework for building and nurturing meaningful relationships that can last a lifetime.

Be Authentic

"You attract what you are"

Be yourself and be genuine in your interactions with others. Authenticity is key to forming lasting friendships. When you showcase who you really are you attract people who are genuinely interest in you and your "real persona". On the other hand, when you try to be someone who you are not you tend to attract superficial people or in general the wrong people into your life.

These superficial connections may not stand the test of time and can leave you feeling unfulfilled. By embracing your true self, you not only attract friends who appreciate you for who you are but also foster deeper and meaningful connections. So, trust in yourself, be authentic, and let your true personality shine – the right friends will be drawn to you naturally.

Practice Self- Care

Take part in activities such as exercise, meditation, or hobbies that bring you joy and relaxation. Pursuing hobbies that bring you joy and relaxation provides a healthy outlet for expressing yourself and taking a break from toxic situations. Whether it's painting, playing music, or trying out a new sport, finding activities that bring you happiness can help you cope with the challenges of dealing with toxic people.

- Here are a few key takeaways from the chapter:
- **Recognize Toxic Behavior**: The first step is to recognize toxic behavior and understand its impact on your well-being. This may include manipulation, constant criticism, or lack of empathy.
- **Set Boundaries**: Establish clear boundaries with toxic individuals to protect your mental and emotional health. Communicate assertively about what behavior is unacceptable to you and stick to those boundaries.
- **Seek Support**: Surround yourself with supportive friends, family members, or campus resources who can provide guidance and validation. Having a strong support system can help you cope with toxic relationships.

- **Limit Contact**: If possible, limit your interactions with toxic individuals or avoid them altogether. This may involve distancing yourself from certain social circles or reducing communication with toxic friends.

- **Focus on Personal Growth**: Use the experience of dealing with toxic people as an opportunity for personal growth and self-reflection. Reflect on what you've learned from these experiences and how you can better protect yourself in the future.

Rachel from University of Rotherham Shared her experience through our Mental health Assistance website- Golads.org. Her article on "Breaking Free: My Journey Away from Toxic Friend Culture" has gained a lot of support and been a motivator to many such college goers to take a step in tackling the "Toxic Culture around them"

Below is the spectacular article written by her.

Read and be Inspired!

During my college days, I found myself entangled in a web of toxic friend culture. At first, it seemed harmless, just a group of friends enjoying each other's company. But as time passed, I began to realize the detrimental effects it was having on my mental health and overall well-being.

It all started innocently enough, with me eager to make friends and find my place in this new environment. I befriended a group of people who seemed fun and outgoing. We spent countless hours together, laughing, studying, and exploring campus. But deep down, there was a hidden problem that I couldn't ignore. The group had a rigid hierarchy, with certain members exerting control and dominance over others. I found myself constantly walking on eggshells, afraid to speak my mind or express my true feelings for fear of being ridiculed or ostracized. It felt like I was constantly being judged, and any deviation from the group's norms was met with scorn and disdain.

As time went on, I began to notice the negative impact this environment was having on me. I became increasingly anxious and insecure, constantly seeking validation from my so-called friends. I was afraid to be myself, afraid to stand up for what I believed in, afraid to rock the boat and risk being cast out from the group.

But deep down, I knew that I couldn't continue living like this. I felt like I deserved better than being put down and controlled by people who said they were my friends. So, feeling really sad and discontented, I made the difficult decision to distance myself from the toxic friend culture that had consumed my college experience.

It wasn't easy. Breaking away from the group meant facing loneliness and uncertainty. But it also meant reclaiming my sense of self-worth and dignity. I began to surround myself with people who uplifted and supported me, rather than tearing me down. I focused on nurturing genuine connections based on mutual respect and understanding.

Slowly but surely, I started to rebuild my confidence and sense of identity. I discovered interests and passions that were truly my own, rather than simply conforming to the expectations of others. And as I forged my own path, I realized that I was stronger and more resilient than I ever thought possible.

Reflecting on my time in college, I am appreciative of the valuable lessons I gained and the growth that has shaped me into who I am today. I may have faced toxic friend culture head-on, but I emerged from the experience with a newfound sense of self-awareness and empowerment. And for that, I'll always be thankful.

The Friendship Thali Approach: A Balanced Plate of Companionship

In the grand feast of college life, friendships are like a well-curated thali—each friend brings a unique flavor, enriching your social experience. A healthy, balanced friendship thali can lead to lasting memories, personal growth, and emotional fulfillment. But just like your food, your social circle needs variety and balance. Let's explore the Friendship Thali Approach in depth, ensuring your social platter stays fulfilling and well-rounded.

The Components of Your Friendship Thali

1. The Core Friend:

Your Dal – This is your go-to, the foundation of your social life, providing consistency and comfort. They're the friend who knows your deepest secrets, stands by you through thick and thin, and helps you through every college mess. Just like dal is a constant in any meal, your core friend is your emotional rock.

2. The Spice Friend:

Your Masala – This friend adds excitement and unpredictability to your life. Whether it's spontaneous road trips, last-minute party plans, or pushing you out of your comfort zone, they spice things up. They make sure your social life never gets boring and bring fun into everyday routines.

3. **The Healthy Friend:**

   Your Salad – This friend is your wellness guide, the one who motivates you to hit the gym, finish assignments, and maintain a healthy lifestyle. They push you to be your best self—physically, mentally, and emotionally. Their influence adds much-needed balance to your often chaotic college life.

4. **The Sweet Friend:**

   Your Dessert – This is the friend who brings kindness and warmth into your life. They are your emotional support system, offering comfort, listening to you without judgment, and showering you with affection when you need it the most. They remind you of life's sweetness, especially during tough times.

5. **The Side Dish Friends:**

   Your Pickles, Chutneys, and Papad – These friends are your casual buddies, project partners, and acquaintances. While they may not be your besties, they add variety to your social circle. Whether it's group study sessions or random hangouts, they bring in fresh perspectives and keep your social life engaging.

The Layered Circle Theory: Who Fits Where?

Now, let's apply a layered circle theory to the Friendship Thali Approach to explain how much time, energy, and importance each type of friend should get in your life.

1. **The Core Circle (Core Friend):**

   This layer is reserved for your closest friend—the one who probably knows you better than anyone else. They deserve a prime spot on your social calendar because they provide the emotional stability you need. It is important to prioritize this relationship, making sure they know how much they mean to you, as they will likely be a long-term part of your life.

2. The Exciting Middle Layer (Spice and Sweet Friends):

This layer is all about keeping your life exciting and emotionally fulfilling. Your spice and sweet friends are key players who make sure you're having fun while also staying grounded. They should get a decent chunk of your time—too much spice can be overwhelming, but just enough will keep life adventurous and heartwarming.

3. The Outer Layer (Healthy Friend and Side Dish Friends):

While the healthy friend plays a crucial role in your growth, their impact doesn't require constant attention. Check in with them regularly for that much-needed push, but don't feel guilty if you don't hang out every day. The same goes for your side dish friends—keep these relationships casual but functional. They're great for maintaining a well-rounded life but don't necessarily need to be front and center.

Balancing Your Friendship Thali

1. Avoid Overloading on One Dish:

Just like you wouldn't pile your thali with only dal, relying too much on one friend is unhealthy. Diversify! Each friend brings a unique strength, and balancing these relationships will make your social life richer and more resilient.

2. **Don't Neglect Any Component**:

   Spending all your time with your core or spice friend can sometimes lead to imbalance. Make time for your healthy and sweet friends too, as they keep you emotionally and physically grounded. Each type of friend deserves attention, just like every dish in a thali completes the meal.

3. **Season Your Thali**:

   Relationships, like food, need seasoning—aka appreciation and care. Be sure to show gratitude, communicate openly, and reciprocate the support your friends give you. A small gesture like a random "thank you" or spending time with them when they need it can go a long way.

4. **Listen to Your Palate**:

   Much like your taste buds tell you when something's off, your instincts will tell you when a friendship isn't healthy anymore. Toxic relationships can drain you emotionally, so don't be afraid to reassess a friendship's place on your thali. Prioritize those who uplift you, support you, and make your life better.

Chapter 3

DILEMMA OF THINKING EVERYONE HAS FIGURED OUT EVERYTHING. THE "COLLEGE ILLUSION"

In the bustling corridors of college campus, you might have a look around and develop a thought everyone around you has their life nearly planned and wrapped up. From the outsider's point of view, it may seem like their paths are perfectly planned out, their goals crystal clear and confidence soaring. All indicating their clear path to success. But as Aesop said *"Appearances can be deceiving"*.

Imagine yourself seated in a lecture hall, encircled by classmates who effortlessly tackle assignments, discuss their post-graduation aspirations with unwavering confidence and carried that confidence in social settings as well, always having a sort of spotlight on them It's only natural in such a setting to question whether you're the sole individual still grappling with the maze of life's uncertainties.

But here is the secret: Not everyone has figured everything out, even they have their hidden struggles, self-doubts and are as clueless as you. They are just better at masking it than you are, remember that.

College frankly speaking isn't about how much your score or how many internships you have under your belt. It more about self-discovery, new experiences, and building yourself bit by bit as you progress. Therefore, assuming that everyone around has figured out their journey is highly unlike and for the most part They Haven't.

How the perceived expectation of having everything figured out in college can create pressure to confirm?

The perceived expectation of having everything figured out in college can be a significant source of pressure for many students. This pressure often stems from societal norms and expectations that suggest college is a time for personal and academic growth, exploration, and ultimately, finding one's path in life. However, this expectation can be unrealistic and overwhelming for many students.

One way this pressure manifests is through the expectation to conform to certain norms or expectations regarding academic performance, career choices, and even extend to their social lives. There's often a belief that students should have a clear plan for their future careers and academic pursuits from the moment they enter college. This can create a sense of urgency and anxiety for those who may not have a clear direction or who may be exploring different options.

As a result, individuals may feel compelled to make decisions that may not align with their true interests or values in order to meet these perceived expectations. For example, a student might choose a major or career path that they believe will lead to financial stability or social approval, even if it doesn't align with their passions or talents. Similarly, they may feel pressured to engage in certain extracurricular activities or social groups that are seen as prestigious or desirable, even if they don't genuinely enjoy them.

The pressure to conform can negatively impact individuals' mental health and general sense of well-being. It can lead to feelings of inadequacy, imposter syndrome, and burnout as students strive to meet unrealistic expectations that may not align with their true selves. Moreover, it can hinder personal growth and exploration, as individuals may feel constrained by the need to fit into a certain mold or meet external standards.

In the long run, succumbing to this pressure can result in a sense of disillusionment and regret as individuals realize they've prioritized external validation over their own happiness and fulfilment. It's important for colleges and universities to recognize and address these pressures by fostering a culture of authenticity, self-discovery, and support for diverse paths and interests. This can involve providing resources for career exploration, promoting a growth mindset, and creating a supportive environment where students feel empowered to pursue their passions and values, even if they don't fit into traditional expectations. Ultimately, by challenging the notion that students need to have everything figured out in college, we can create a more inclusive and fulfilling educational experience for all.

<u>How Lack of Authentic connections is a side effect of assuming that everyone in college has everything figured out.</u>

Let's talk about the obvious first the fear factor. Assuming everyone has figured out the perfect blueprint of the future means having the fear of being judged for admitting that they are lost or are uncertain on things. They will be viewed as inferior or flawed by his/her peers. Moreover, they might always be on their guard protection their social image and avoid seeking help or support when needed and this can cause individuals to isolate themselves and prevent them from building connections based on authenticity and meaning. Moreover, as you create a "fake persona" in order to fit and pretend to be someone you are not, you develop superficial relationships with your peers instead of genuine connections that last a lifetime. Such superficial relationships cause emotions drain, and mental distress in the long-term arising from factors such as relationship built on false pretenses, lack of support and understanding between counterparts. It's always helpful to be as authentic as possible and avoid narrow beliefs that might arise from your nonconscious telling you to "fit in" and avoid being the weird one out.

Imposter Syndrome: The "Mujhse Na Ho Paayega" Feeling

Ever feel like you're *winging it* in life and someone's going to point at you and say, *"Yeh toh bas chori-chupe aa gaya yahaan tak"?* Despite all your hard work, you somehow feel like you have just stumbled your way here while everyone else seems to have their life together.

Welcome to the not-so-fun world of **Imposter Syndrome**! It's that constant sense of *"Yaar, how did I even get here?"*—where you're convinced, you're way out of your depth, surrounded by *real* smart people, while you're just... surviving.

Even if you have racked up some major wins, imposter syndrome will have you downplaying it, attributing your success to pure luck, or your horoscope (*"Arre yaar, aaj ka din achha tha bas!"*). Meanwhile, you're living in fear that someone will find out you're not as capable as you appear. It's like you're starring in your own episode of *Kaun Banega Imposter?*

How it Sneaks Up on You

- **Downplaying Your Achievements**: Scored well in exams? *"Yaar, bas paper easy tha!"* Landed that internship everyone wanted? "*Oh, bas connection ka kamaal tha.*" Never mind the hours of effort you put in—you've convinced yourself it's just dumb luck.

- **Fear of Being "Found Out"**: Ever have that "*Koi na koi toh pakad lega*" feeling? Like any moment someone's going to tell you, "*Acha yeh? Yeh bas galti se pass ho gaya!*" when like you have worked hard. Yeah, that's imposter syndrome whispering in your ear.

- **Comparing Yourself to Everyone Else**: Whether it's your college topper or the person who never studies and still aces every exam (*kyun bhai, kaise?*), imposter syndrome has you convinced they're doing everything right while you're just one bad grade away from disaster.

So, What Can You Do? *Tension Mat Lo!*

1. **Acknowledge Your Feelings**: Step one—realize you're not the only one with these doubts. Even top students and professionals have those *'What if I'm not good enough?"* moments. Just knowing that can make imposter syndrome lose some of its power.

2. **Reframe Negative Thoughts**: Instead of letting your brain go all *'Mujhse na ho paayega,"* try shifting the narrative to *'Wait, I've done this before, I can do it again."* Focus on what you're good at. After all, you didn't reach here by just luck and *aashirwad* from the stars.

3. **Set Realistic Goals**: Sometimes you set goals that even superheroes would struggle with. Break them down into bite-sized tasks. And don't forget to reward yourself after ticking

off even the small wins—yes, even that one extra reading you managed to do!

4. **Seek Support**: Talk to someone—whether it's a friend, family member, or a counselor. Sharing your thoughts can help you realize that everyone, yes even *Sharma ji ka beta*, has their moments of doubt.

5. **Focus on Learning**: Don't worry about proving your worth. College is about learning, not being perfect. Treat every challenge as a chance to grow, not as a judgment on your competence. You're here to learn, not win the *Student of the Year* award, okay?

6. **Practice Self-Compassion**: When things don't go your way, be kind to yourself. Remember, even superheroes mess up sometimes, and guess what? So can you! Take a breather, laugh it off, and move forward. *Tension mat lo!*

7. **Limit Social Comparison**: Constantly comparing yourself to others—especially on social media—is like playing a game you can't win. Instead, focus on *your* journey. Social media highlights people's best moments, not their struggles. You're doing great, even if your life doesn't look Instagram-perfect.

8. **Keep a Journal**: Write down what you're feeling. Seriously, when you see those thoughts on paper, they'll seem less daunting. Plus, it's a good way to track your progress. Trust me, you'll look back and say, *"Arre, I've actually come far!"*

9. **Celebrate Achievements**: Whether it's a small win or a big one, celebrate it! If you managed to sit through an entire

3-hour lecture, pat yourself on the back. Every step forward counts, so don't be shy about giving yourself some credit.

Recognizing that learning is a lifelong journey and understanding that it's okay not to have all the answers right away allows individuals to embrace the learning process fully. It reduces the fear of failure and encourages experimentation and exploration.

College is termed as your transformative years for a reason, here multiple factors shape your personality, thought process and ambitions for the future and there it is impossible for anyone to figured out everything. It's not Humanly possible. Some might have a plan ready but 99% of time there are major changes done to this so called "perfect plan" through college and even extending to your young adulthood. Therefore, not having answers to each question life throws at you urges an individual to Embrace change and learn, it encourages a continuous process of growth and development throughout life.

Embarking on your college journey is more than just an academic endeavor; it's a profound opportunity for personal growth and self-discovery. At the heart of this transformative experience is the cultivation of a growth mindset, the courage to embrace vulnerability, and a redefinition of what it means to be successful. This chapter will guide you through these concepts, blending motivational insights with actionable advice, illuminated by the stories of individuals who have walked this path before you. Prepare to unlock your potential, overcome obstacles, and reshape your definition of success, setting the foundation for a fulfilling college experience and beyond.

Understanding the Growth Mindset

The Core of a Growth Mindset

Coined by psychologist Carol Dweck, the concept of a growth mindset revolves around the belief that talents and abilities are not static traits but can be nurtured through effort, persistence, and intentional practice. This perspective stands in contrast to a fixed mindset, where individuals view their capacities as rigid, predetermined limits. Such a belief system often leads to an aversion to risk, a fear of failure, and a reluctance to engage in challenging tasks.

Adopting a growth mindset profoundly influences how students confront academic, social, and personal challenges. Instead of viewing obstacles as insurmountable, students with a growth mindset see these difficulties as stepping stones toward development. The focus shifts from an overwhelming fear of failure to the understanding that learning—often messy and imperfect—is the true path to mastery. This mindset not only enhances academic performance but also fosters personal growth and enriches relationships, encouraging a more holistic approach to success that extends beyond grades and accolades.

Nurturing a Growth Mindset

Fostering a growth mindset within the high-pressure environment of college necessitates a deliberate realignment of goals, attitudes, and actions. The key lies in reframing objectives. Rather than focusing on external markers of success—such as achieving top grades or outshining peers—students should anchor their efforts in learning-oriented goals that emphasize personal progress, skill development, and intellectual exploration.

View challenges as opportunities for refinement: College rigor is designed to push the boundaries of your intellectual capabilities. Instead of avoiding challenges, recognize that grappling with difficult problems enhances creativity, problem-solving skills, and resilience. Challenges are the crucibles where growth is forged.

Build resilience in the face of setbacks: Failure is inevitable on the path to success, but students with a growth mindset understand that setbacks are not reflections of personal inadequacy. Instead, these individuals analyze mistakes, learn from them, and adjust their approaches, transforming adversity into a vehicle for growth.

Reframe effort as the foundation of mastery: In a culture that often glorifies effortless success, it is easy to see hard work as a sign of deficiency. However, from the perspective of a growth mindset, effort is not a weakness but the driving force behind improvement. Through sustained, purposeful effort, students can master even the most complex subjects and skills.

Welcome constructive feedback as a means for growth: Receiving criticism, especially when it highlights areas for improvement, can be difficult. However, those who embrace a growth mindset recognize that feedback—when offered constructively—provides an invaluable opportunity to refine skills and deepen understanding. Engaging with feedback fosters continuous improvement and cultivates humility.

Celebrate incremental progress : Growth is often a gradual process, and its signs may not always be immediately apparent. Acknowledging and celebrating small victories is crucial for maintaining motivation and sustaining a sense of accomplishment, particularly when working on long-term projects or pursuing ambitious goals.

The Transformative Impact of a Growth Mindset in College

Adopting a growth mindset in college not only enhances academic performance but also reshapes the broader definition of success. Rather than relying solely on traditional measures such as grades or awards, students are encouraged to cultivate a more profound sense of achievement—one that is deeply rooted in self-improvement, curiosity, and intellectual humility.

Ultimately, a growth mindset transforms the college experience into a journey of personal evolution, where learning becomes a lifelong pursuit of self-betterment and adaptability. With this mindset, the scope for growth—academically and personally—becomes boundless, and students are empowered to navigate the complexities of life with confidence and purpose.

The Power of Embracing Vulnerability - Expanding the Definition of Success

In the pursuit of knowledge and personal development, vulnerability is not a weakness but a profound strength. Embracing vulnerability means admitting you don't have all the answers, being open to new experiences, and acknowledging your fears and uncertainties. This openness is crucial in college, where the learning process is as much about discovering yourself as it is about acquiring academic knowledge.

Brené Brown's Insights on Vulnerability-

Brené Brown, a research professor known for her studies on vulnerability, courage, empathy, and shame, brought the power of vulnerability to the forefront of public consciousness. Her viral

TED talk and subsequent works argue that vulnerability is the birthplace of innovation, creativity, and change. For college students, Brown's message underscores the importance of stepping out of your comfort zone, engaging deeply with your peers and your studies, and embracing the discomfort that often accompanies learning and growth.

Strategies to Embrace Vulnerability in College

- <u>Ask for Help</u>: Recognize that asking for help is a sign of strength, not weakness. Whether it's academic support or mental health resources, seeking assistance is a step
- toward growth.
- <u>Share Your Experiences</u>: Open up to peers about your challenges and successes. This not only builds deeper connections but also creates a supportive community where vulnerability is valued.
- <u>Take Risks:</u> Engage in activities and courses outside your comfort zone. The risk of failure is often outweighed by the potential for significant personal and
- academic growth.

Traditionally, success in college has been narrowly defined by grades, test scores, and degree attainment. While these are important milestones, they don't encompass the full spectrum of what it means to be successful. True success also involves personal growth, resilience, forming meaningful relationships, and contributing to your community. Redefining success involves setting and striving for goals that are personally meaningful and reflective of your values and aspirations.

Crafting Your Unique Definition of Success

- **Identify Your Values and Passions:** Reflect on what is genuinely important to you. Success is deeply personal, and understanding your values and passions is the first step toward defining it on your own terms.

- **Set Holistic Goals:** Beyond academic achievements, set goals related to personal development, such as improving communication skills, building a diverse and supportive network, or contributing to a cause you care about.

- **Embrace the Journey:** Recognize that success is not a destination but a journey. Celebrate your progress and the lessons learned along the way, even if the path deviates from your initial plans.

Redefining success in college requires a shift in perspective from viewing success as a checklist of achievements to understanding it as a holistic journey of growth, learning, and contribution. By embracing a growth mindset, acknowledging vulnerability, and setting personal and meaningful goals, you can create a fulfilling college experience that prepares you for a successful life beyond academia.

Reading Suggestions:

For readers interested in delving deeper into the themes of cultivating a growth mindset, embracing vulnerability, and redefining success, especially within the context of college life and beyond, the following books offer a wealth of insights, strategies, and inspiration. Each selection complements the topics discussed in the chapter, providing readers with a broader understanding and practical tools to apply these concepts in their own lives.

- "Mindset: The New Psychology of Success" by Carol S. Dweck - This foundational book by psychologist Carol Dweck explores the concept of the "fixed" vs. "growth" mindset. Dweck's research demonstrates how our beliefs about our abilities affect every aspect of our lives and how adopting a growth mindset can lead to greater
- success and fulfillment.
- "Daring Greatly: How the Courage to Be Vulnerable Transforms the Way We Live, Love, Parent, and Lead" by Brené Brown - In this powerful book, Brené Brown examines the importance of vulnerability in creating strong connections, fostering innovation, and living a full, authentic life. Brown's insights are particularly relevant for college students navigating new challenges and relationships.
- "How to Fail at Almost Everything and Still Win Big: Kind of the Story of My Life" by Scott Adams - Dilbert creator Scott Adams shares his personal journey of failures and lessons learned, leading to eventual success. Adams's humorous and insightful book offers a unique perspective on how to view failures as valuable learning experiences rather than setbacks, aligning well with the concept of a growth mindset.

Chapter 4

CAMPUS ZEN: MASTERING MENTAL HEALTH IN COLLEGE

The TALK

Let's talk about mental health. I know it's still a taboo subject, and many people would rather suffer in silence than open up about it. Maybe society just isn't ready. Mental health is a topic very close to me. During mid-2020, in the height of COVID, I was not doing well mentally—the stress, the uncertainty. I had just graduated from 12th grade and had no clue what to do next. I also had my fair share of anxiety growing up, and everything just piled up during that time. The sleepless nights, the constant unease about nothing in particular—I felt like I was a disease without a cure.

At that point, I started doing a lot of research about mental health, and gradually, I gained more control over it. I realized I was not alone. There were so many teenagers caught in this cycle of depression, and the effects of COVID only made it worse. I knew I had to do something.

That's how golads.org was born—one evening over a conference call with a few friends. We started a mental health organization to provide comprehensive support for mental health seekers. We offer everything from DIY tools and helpful resources to live chat support, and we pioneered an interest-based therapy approach. Golads connects young people with mental health counsellors and organizes events to empower them.

(For more information, visit our website. At Golads, we're always here for you, especially when you feel like you're all alone. Because mental health matters—your mental health matters.)

The Art of Saying No

Navigating college life is like walking through a minefield of invitations, requests, and opportunities. It's a whirlwind of social gatherings, academic pursuits, and extracurricular activities. In the midst of this chaos, the art of saying no becomes a crucial skill to master. It's not just about declining invitations; it's about setting boundaries, managing time effectively, and prioritizing your well-being.

One of the fundamental concepts underlying the art of saying no is the idea of prioritization. In college, there's a constant tug-of-war between academic responsibilities and social engagements. While it's tempting to say yes to every party, outing, or club meeting, it's important to recognize the value of your time and energy. Prioritizing commitments means evaluating each opportunity based on its significance to your overall goals and well-being.

Psychologist William Ury, in his book "The Power of a Positive No," introduces the concept of the "positive no" as a way to assertively decline requests while maintaining respect and integrity. Instead of a blunt rejection, a positive no involves three steps: first, acknowledging the request or invitation; second, stating your refusal clearly and without apology; and third, offering an alternative or explanation, if necessary. This approach allows you to assert your boundaries while preserving relationships and fostering understanding.

Another aspect of the art of saying no is understanding the difference between assertiveness and aggression. Assertiveness involves expressing your needs and preferences in a clear and respectful manner, without infringing on the rights of others. Aggression, on the other hand, is forceful and hostile, often disregarding the feelings or perspectives of others. By mastering assertiveness, you can confidently decline invitations or requests without feeling guilty or confrontational.

Setting boundaries is another essential aspect of the art of saying no. Boundaries define the limits of what is acceptable and unacceptable in terms of how others treat us and how we treat ourselves. Establishing healthy boundaries means knowing when to say no to requests, invitations, or behaviors that compromise our well-being, values, or personal boundaries. This might involve declining social invitations when you need time to recharge, saying no to additional commitments when your plate is already full, or asserting yourself in situations where your boundaries are being violated.

Learning to say no also requires self-awareness and self-compassion. It's important to recognize your limitations and honor your needs, whether they're academic, social, or emotional. Saying no doesn't make you selfish or uncaring; it's a form of self-care that allows you to protect your time, energy, and mental health. Remember, it's okay to prioritize yourself and your well-being.

Practicing mindfulness can also enhance your ability to say no effectively. By staying present in the moment and tuning into your thoughts and feelings, you can make decisions that align with your values and goals. Mindfulness can help you discern between genuine opportunities and distractions, allowing you to say no with confidence and clarity.

In conclusion, the art of saying no is an essential skill for college students navigating the myriad demands of academic and social life. By prioritizing commitments, mastering assertiveness, practicing self-awareness, and embracing mindfulness, you can confidently decline invitations and requests while maintaining respect and integrity. Remember, saying no isn't about closing doors; it's about opening yourself to opportunities that truly align with your goals and values.

Instagram reels - how Instagram algorithm is your biggest enemy of your metal health

The allure of Instagram reels lies in their endless scrollability and bite-sized content. From dance challenges to cooking tutorials, there's something for everyone. However, beneath the surface, lies an algorithm meticulously designed to keep users hooked for as long as possible. It operates on the principle of engagement, serving up content based on what it thinks will generate the most likes, comments, and shares. This means that the more time you spend scrolling, the more the algorithm learns about your preferences, creating a feedback loop that can be difficult to break.

One of the key theories at play here is the concept of variable rewards, straight out of B.F. Skinner's playbook. You know, the guy with the rats and the lever? Yeah, that one. Every time you open Instagram, you're essentially pulling that lever, hoping for a juicy reward in the form of a hilarious reel or a mesmerizing dance routine. And just like Skinner's rats, you never know when that reward will come, keeping you perpetually hooked and coming back for more.

But wait, there's more! Enter the concept of social comparison theory, courtesy of the one and only Leon Festinger. This gem of a theory suggests that humans have an innate tendency to compare themselves to others, particularly when it comes to social media. And boy, does Instagram reel in the comparisons like a pro angler reeling in a big catch. Whether it's that influencer with the perfect beach body or that friend who seems to be living their best life 24/7, it's easy to fall into the trap of feeling inadequate in comparison.

In the context of college life, where stress levels are already at an all-time high, the constant barrage of curated content can exacerbate feelings of inadequacy and comparison. You see your classmates posting about their latest achievements, their picture-perfect study sessions, and their seemingly endless social lives, and suddenly, your own accomplishments pale in comparison. It's easy to fall into the trap of measuring your self-worth based on likes and followers, forgetting that social media is merely a highlight reel of someone else's life.

This is where the art of saying no comes into play, in a digital context. Just as we must learn to say no to unnecessary commitments and obligations in real life, we must also learn to set boundaries with social media. It's about recognizing when to step away from the endless scroll and reclaim control over our time and attention. Instead of mindlessly consuming content that leaves us feeling drained and inadequate, we can choose to engage with platforms intentionally, seeking out content that uplifts and inspires us.

But here's the catch: the Instagram algorithm is programmed to keep us scrolling for as long as possible, constantly bombarding us with new content tailored to our interests. It's a never-ending cycle of consumption that can feel impossible to escape. However, by understanding how the algorithm works, we can outsmart it and reclaim our mental health.

One strategy is to limit our exposure to Instagram reels altogether. This doesn't mean abandoning the platform entirely but rather setting boundaries around when and how we engage with it. Perhaps it means allocating a specific time each day for scrolling or using features like the mute button to filter out content that doesn't serve us. It's about taking back control of our digital habits and prioritizing our well-being above all else.

Of course, this is easier said than done, especially for college students who are constantly bombarded with notifications and peer pressure to stay connected. It requires a conscious effort to resist the lure of the algorithm and prioritize our mental health. But with practice and perseverance, it is possible to find a balance between staying informed and staying sane in the digital age.

In my own experience, I've found that setting boundaries with social media has been instrumental in preserving my mental health during college. By being intentional about when and how I engage with platforms like Instagram, I've been able to create a healthier relationship with technology and prioritize activities that bring me joy and fulfillment. And while the Instagram algorithm may continue to evolve and adapt, I take comfort in knowing that I have the power to control how I interact with it.

BUILDING RESILIENCE, EMBRACING JUGAAD

Ah, – it's like the hero's theme song playing in the background of your life's montage, lurging you to rise above every setback with dramatic flair! In our beloved Bollywood movies, resilience isn't just a trait; it's a full-blown spectacle, complete with tear-jerking dialogues, gravity-defying stunts, and, of course, the obligatory song and dance sequence.

Now, let's translate this larger-than-life resilience into the chaotic world of an Indian college student. Imagine you've just received your exam results, and instead of the glorious victory march you had envisioned, it's more of a stumble through a landmine of red marks and disappointment. Cue the melodramatic music!

In true Bollywood fashion, resilience kicks in like a superhero's grand entrance. You wipe away those tears of frustration, stand up straight, and declare to the universe (or maybe just to your mirror), "I will not be defeated!" It's the moment when you channel the spirit of every on-screen hero who's faced insurmountable odds and emerged victorious, often with a killer one-liner and a stylish hair flick.

But here's where the magic happens – in Bollywood, resilience isn't just about stubbornly refusing to accept defeat; it's about turning setbacks into opportunities for epic comebacks. So, instead of wallowing in self-pity, you hit the books with renewed determination, fueled by the belief that the climax of your story is yet to come.

And just like in our favorite movies, where the hero's journey is sprinkled with mentors, allies, and unexpected twists, your journey through college is also peppered with moments of support and serendipity. Whether it's a timely pep talk from a friend, a stroke of inspiration from a random lecture, or a plot twist that leads you down a surprising path, resilience means being open to the universe's plot twists and trusting that they'll ultimately lead you to your happy ending.

So, the next time you find yourself face-to-face with failure, don't just see it as the end of the road; see it as the turning point in your blockbuster saga. Cue the dramatic music, summon your inner Bollywood hero, and remember: resilience isn't just a trait – it's your ticket to a plot twist-filled journey of growth and triumph!

Ah, the Jugaad Philosophy – the quintessential Indian approach to problem-solving that's as ingenious as it is unconventional. In a country where chaos reigns supreme and "adjust kar lenge" is practically our national motto, jugaad isn't just a skill; it's a way of life.

Imagine you're faced with a seemingly insurmountable challenge – maybe you forgot about a major assignment until the night before it's due, or perhaps your laptop decides to go on strike right in the middle of exam season. In moments like these, mere mortals might panic, but not you, oh no! You're a practitioner of the Jugaad Philosophy, which means you thrive in the midst of chaos and uncertainty.

So, what exactly is jugaad? Well, it's the art of finding quick, creative, and often unconventional solutions to problems, using whatever resources happen to be at hand. It's about thinking outside the box, breaking the rules (just a little), and embracing the spirit of innovation in all its glorious forms.

In the context of college life, jugaad can take many forms. Maybe you forgot to study for a test, but instead of resigning yourself to failure, you quickly form a study group with your classmates and pool your collective knowledge (and panic) to cram as much information as possible into your sleep-deprived brain. Or perhaps you're struggling to make ends meet on a shoestring budget, so you get creative with your cooking, turning leftovers into gourmet meals worthy of a five-star restaurant (or at least a two-star hostel canteen).

But jugaad isn't just about making do with what you have; it's about turning limitations into opportunities and obstacles into stepping stones. It's about embracing the chaos of college life and finding beauty in the messiness of it all. Because let's face it – life rarely goes according to plan, and sometimes the best solutions are the ones you never saw coming.

So, the next time you find yourself staring down a seemingly impossible task, don't panic – embrace the chaos, unleash your inner jugaadu, and remember: where there's a will (and a little bit of jugaad), there's always a way!

1. Embrace the Chaos

Picture this: it's the night before exams, and you haven't even touched your textbooks. Panic mode: activated! But hey, who needs sleep anyway? Embrace the chaos, my friend. Jugaad is all about thriving in the midst of madness. So, grab that pile of notes, brew another cup of chai, and dive headfirst into the abyss. Remember, it's not about how well you prepare; it's about how gracefully you navigate the storm.

Personal Experience: I once found myself cramming an entire semester's worth of material into one night. Did I ace the exam? Well, let's just say I passed with flying colors – and a newfound appreciation for last-minute miracles.

2. Turn Problems into Opportunities

Life throws lemons at you? Time to make some lemonade – with a desi twist, of course! In the world of Jugaad, problems are just opportunities in disguise. Can't afford fancy study materials? No worries! Get creative with what you have. Old newspapers, cereal boxes, and a dash of imagination – voila! You've got yourself DIY study aids that would make MacGyver proud.

Humorous Insight: Who needs expensive textbooks when you have Google, Wikipedia, and that one friend who never misses a lecture? Ah, the perks of being a broke college student!

3. Learn to Laugh at Yourself

Let's face it – we've all had our fair share of epic fails and embarrassing moments. But hey, laughter is the best medicine, right? Embrace the absurdity of it all, and don't be afraid to laugh at yourself. From slipping on banana peels to accidentally sending love letters to the professor instead of your crush – we've been there, done that. And you know what? It makes for some great stories!

Personal Anecdote: I once pulled an all-nighter studying for a test, only to realize it was scheduled for the following week. Classic case of "better safe than sorry," right? Let's just say I became a pro at binge-watching Netflix that night.

4. Find Strength in Community

They say it takes a village to raise a child – well, it takes a squad to survive college! Your fellow students are your greatest allies in the battlefield of academia. Form study groups, share notes, and commiserate over the horrors of midterms together. In the world of Jugaad, strength lies in numbers. Plus, misery loves company, right?

Humorous Insight: Ever been part of a group project where everyone disappears until the night before the deadline? Ah, the joys of teamwork – or lack thereof. But hey, nothing brings people together like the fear of failing, am I right?

5. Celebrate Small Victories

In the midst of all the chaos and craziness, don't forget to celebrate the little wins. Whether it's acing a quiz, surviving a particularly brutal lecture, or simply making it through the day without falling asleep in class – every victory counts. Treat yourself to some well-deserved samosas, indulge in a Netflix binge, or dance like nobody's watching (preferably after locking your room door).

Personal Anecdote: I once wrote an entire essay using only memes as references. Did I get an A+? Not quite. But did I make my professor laugh? Absolutely! Sometimes, it's the small victories that bring the most joy.

Embracing Loneliness: The Art of Finding Peace Within.

- *The Sanctuary Theory.*

In essence, the Sanctuary Theory posits that loneliness isn't just an absence of company; it's an opportunity to create a sacred space within oneself, a sanctuary amidst the chaos of life. This theory draws inspiration from the concept of solitude as a refuge, a place where one can retreat from the demands of the external world and find solace in their own company. In the quietude of solitude, we have the opportunity to connect with our innermost thoughts, feelings, and desires. We can listen to the whispers of our intuition, untangle the knots of our emotions, and rediscover the essence of who we truly are.

Imagine loneliness as not just an empty room, but a room filled with possibilities. It's like stumbling upon a hidden garden in the midst of a bustling city – a tranquil oasis where you can escape the noise and chaos of everyday life. Instead of viewing loneliness as a negative state to be avoided at all costs, why not embrace it as an invitation to create your own sanctuary?

Practically speaking, embracing the Sanctuary Theory involves cultivating a mindset of acceptance and appreciation for solitude. Rather than resisting or resenting moments of loneliness, see them as opportunities for self-reflection, introspection, and rejuvenation.

- Create Sacred Spaces

Think of a sacred space as your personal hideout from all the chaos. Set up a cozy spot with a comfy chair, fairy lights, and maybe some posters of your Netflix show, Anime or Sitcoms like *friends or big bang theory*, whatever your comfort show might be. This will be your go-to place when you need to escape from your academic stress, personal problems or even your roommate's snoring. Remember this is your "Me spot" so keep thought about anything or anyone that might stress you out as far as possible before entering.

- Practice Self-Care

Self-care isn't just for weekends, folks. Picture this: you, a face mask (yes even guys it's not a taboo to indulge in some skin care once in a while) and your favorite Bollywood playlist. Whether it's a just a long shower without interruptions or treating yourself to your favorite biryani, or just zoning out with some deep breaths, make time for you. Remember, calories don't count when you're treating yourself.

- Engage in Mindfulness

Yes, mindfulness. Not just a fancy word your yoga teacher uses. Here's how you can do it without feeling like a monk:

Breathing Exercises: When your lecturer goes on and on about something you don't understand, practice deep breathing. Inhale the positive vibes, exhale the confusion.

Meditation App: There are tons of apps that can guide you. Plus, you can do it sitting on your bed with your pajamas on. No need for those tight yoga pants.

o *MindMap Therapy (Congnitive behavioural theory)*

is like having a personal mental gym trainer, focusing on the connection between your thoughts, feelings, and behaviors. It works on the idea that what we think about ourselves, others, and the world influences how we feel and act. By spotting and challenging those pesky negative thoughts, CBT helps us make positive changes in our behavior and emotional well-being. Let's break down how it works, Indian college style:

1. Spotting Thought Patterns: Imagine your mind is a WhatsApp chat group, and automatic thoughts are those random messages that pop up without warning. They can be rational or irrational, but they have a huge impact on your mood and actions. For instance, if you bomb a test (thanks, engineering), you might think, "I'm useless" or "My future is ruined."

2. Catching Cognitive Distortions: CBT helps you catch those annoying cognitive distortions – basically, your brain's version of fake news. Here are a few:

1. All-or-nothing thinking: Seeing things in black and white, like "I have to get a 10 CGPA or I'm a failure."
2. Overgeneralization: Making sweeping statements based on one incident, like "I got rejected once, so no one will ever like me."
3. - Catastrophizing: Expecting the worst, like "If I don't get an internship, my career is over."
4. Personalization: Taking on blame for things you can't control, like "The group project failed because of me."

3. <u>Reframing Thoughts:</u> *Once you've identified these distortions, CBT teaches you to challenge and reframe them. It's like giving your brain a reality check. Question the evidence for and against your thought, look at alternatives, and find more balanced responses. Instead of thinking, "I'm a failure," remind yourself of your past achievements and consider other factors that might have affected your performance.

4. <u>Behavioral Activation:</u> Besides mental gymnastics, CBT gets you to flex your action muscles. Set specific goals, break tasks into baby steps, and face your fears (like asking that crush out) gradually. By taking these steps, you'll feel more accomplished and in control.

5. <u>Building Skills and Coping Strategies:</u> CBT is like a life skills class. It teaches you relaxation techniques, problem-solving skills, assertiveness, and communication. These skills help you handle stress and setbacks, making you more resilient and less impacted by negative thoughts.

Overall, CBT is a team effort, where you actively participate and develop the skills to manage and overcome psychological challenges. By exploring thought patterns, challenging distortions, and using behavioral strategies, CBT helps you break free from negative cycles and boost your mental health. So, consider it a mental workout plan – it might just be the thing you need to navigate the rollercoaster of college life.

The Power of Journaling: More Than Just Scribbles

Journaling—what's the big deal, right? It's just putting your thoughts on paper, something you might have done in school with a diary that you hid from your siblings. But in college, journaling can be so much more. It's not just a way to vent about that annoying group member who never shows up for meetings or the professor who thinks his subject is the only one you're taking. It's a powerful tool for managing stress, tracking progress, and fostering creativity.

There are different types of journaling that you can explore, depending on what you need.

Bullet Journals: Perfect for those who like structure. It's a combination of a to-do list, diary, and planner. The best part? You can customize it as much as you want. Add doodles, motivational quotes, or even track your mood and sleep patterns. For the perfectionist in you, a bullet journal is like a playground where you can organize your life with flair.

Reflective Journals: This is where you can pour your heart out. Reflect on your day, your interactions, your achievements, and your failures. It's a safe space to analyze your thoughts and feelings, helping you understand yourself better. It's like having a conversation with your inner self, only this time, you're actually listening.

Gratitude Journal : These are all about focusing on the positive. In a sea of assignments and deadlines, it's easy to lose sight of the good things. A gratitude journal helps you keep track of what you're thankful for, no matter how small. Did you find a seat on the metro during rush hour? Write it down! Managed to get through a tough exam? That's another entry. Over time, you'll start seeing the brighter side of college life, even on the toughest days.

The benefits of journaling go beyond just keeping a record of your thoughts. For an Indian college student, it's a way to manage the overwhelming pressure that comes with academics and social life. Journaling can help reduce stress by allowing you to express your feelings freely, without the fear of judgment. It's also a great way to track your academic progress. Whether it's noting down the topics you need to revise or reflecting on how you handled a particularly tricky assignment, journaling helps you stay on top of your game.

Starting a journal might seem daunting, but it doesn't have to be perfect. The key is consistency. Set aside a few minutes each day to jot down your thoughts. Don't worry about grammar or spelling—this is for your eyes only. Over time, you'll find that journaling becomes a habit, one that you look forward to at the end of a long day.

Of course, journaling isn't without its challenges. There will be days when you'll stare at a blank page, unsure of what to write. And that's okay. Sometimes, the act of just putting pen to paper is enough. You might end up doodling more than writing, but that's all part of the process. After all, it's your journal—there are no rules.

A word of caution: journaling can become addictive. You might find yourself filling up notebooks faster than you can buy them, or spending more time decorating your bullet journal than actually studying. But hey, if it helps you stay organized and sane, who's complaining?

Integrating Journaling and Scheduling: A Winning Combination

let's talk about how these two practices can work together to create a powerful system for acing college life. On their own, journaling and scheduling are effective tools, but when combined, they can take your productivity and well-being to the next level.

Journaling can be a great companion to your scheduling efforts. For instance, at the end of each day, you can use your journal to reflect on how well you stuck to your schedule. Did you manage to complete all your tasks? If not, what were the obstacles? This reflection helps you identify patterns in your behavior, such as procrastination triggers or times of the day when you're most productive. Over time, this self-awareness allows you to adjust your schedule to better suit your needs.

Moreover, journaling gives you a space to celebrate your victories, no matter how small. Did you finally manage to wake up at 6 AM for that study session? Write it down! These small wins add up and can be incredibly motivating, especially during stressful times like exam season.

On the flip side, your schedule can inform your journaling practice. As you plan out your week, set aside specific times for journaling. This ensures that it becomes a regular habit, rather than something you do only when you remember or when you're feeling particularly stressed. You can also use your schedule to track your journaling goals, such as writing a certain number of entries each week or exploring different types of journaling.

But the benefits of combining journaling and scheduling go beyond just productivity. Together, they help you maintain a balanced life. While your schedule keeps you on track with your academic and social commitments, your journal provides an outlet for your thoughts and feelings. This balance is crucial for maintaining mental health, something that often gets overlooked in the hustle and bustle of college life.

In practice, this combination might look something like this: You start your day by reviewing your schedule and setting your intentions for the day. As you go through your tasks, you jot down quick notes in your journal—maybe a reminder to follow up on an assignment, or a reflection on how you handled a difficult conversation with a classmate. At the end of the day, you revisit your journal to reflect on what went well and what could have gone better. You might also adjust your schedule for the next day based on what you've learned.

And let's not forget the satisfaction of checking off tasks from your schedule and filling up pages in your journal. There's something incredibly rewarding about seeing your progress in tangible form, whether it's a completed to-do list or a journal full of thoughts and reflections. It's a reminder that, despite the challenges, you're moving forward.

Of course, no system is perfect. There will be days when you're too tired to journal or when your schedule goes completely out the window. But that's okay. The goal isn't perfection; it's progress. By consistently practicing journaling and scheduling, you'll develop habits that will serve you well not just in college, but in life beyond.

So, embrace these tools, and don't be afraid to make them your own. Whether you prefer digital apps or pen and paper, the important thing is to find what works for you and stick with it. And who knows? You might just find that these practices not only help you ace college but also make the journey a lot more enjoyable.

Chapter 5
RED FLAG GREEN FLAG: LOVE UNFILTERED

Falling in love as a young adult, especially in college, feels like navigating a minefield of confusion, expectations, and, more often than not, disappointment. I mean, let's be real—when you step onto campus for the first time, you're greeted by a flood of people who are more interested in swiping right on Tinder than swiping right on your soul. And that's just the beginning. Dating in college feels like trying to find a Wi-Fi signal in the basement: confusing, exhausting, and most of the time, you don't even know if you're connected properly. I'm from India, so naturally, there is the added spice of balancing expectations from your family (who still think you should only date someone they pick) and the ultra-modern hookup culture that's all about speed, fun, and forgetting your own name by morning.

The thing is, this generation is all about instant gratification. From food delivery apps to binge-watching an entire TV series in one night, patience is not exactly our virtue. And that, unfortunately, spills over into our dating lives. Relationships these days are like a Netflix trial—free for a month, but then, you know, you start to lose interest or feel like it's too much commitment to actually pay for it. I get it, we're all young, free, and drowning in assignments, but somewhere between late-night texts that go nowhere and endless 'situationships,' you start wondering: when did falling in love become so transactional? When did it stop being about forming deep bonds and become all about how fast you can update your Instagram bio to include someone else's initials?

Being in college makes it worse. You're surrounded by the constant pressure to keep things casual because "nobody wants to be tied down" during the so-called best years of their life. It's the era of "I like you, but not enough to stop seeing other people," or the classic, "Let's keep things fun and light—no need for labels." And that would be fine if we weren't human beings with actual feelings. But no, one day you're doing fine, cruising through life, and the next day you're ghosted because apparently, ghosting is the only way people break up these days. Forget conversations about emotions or explanations. Nah, just vanish like the 4GB data I thought would last the entire week.

The sad part is, college is actually the time when many of us could benefit from learning what a healthy, committed relationship feels like. It is a critical stage in life when you're figuring out who you are, what you want, and how to deal with the complexities of adult life. Relationships, if taken seriously, could help you grow. They could teach you compromise, patience, empathy, and how to make space for someone else in your life while still trying to juggle classes, internships, and, in my case, the constant pressure of acing my GMATs but no, what do we get instead? We get fleeting moments of 'fun' where people are more interested in adding another body to their list than actually getting to know what your favorite book is, or, you know, what you want to do in life.

The irony is that while we chase this temporary pleasure, deep down, most of us crave something more substantial. We want someone to call at 2 AM when the stress of life is too much to handle, not just someone to share a late-night party with. We want someone who is there for the long haul, who's interested in more than just a quick fling. But that's where the struggle lies. In this generation, commitment is seen as a four-letter word. The minute you start talking about the future or about something meaningful, people hit the panic button. Like, "Whoa, whoa, I didn't sign up for emotional investment. Can we just, like, have fun?"

As an Indian student, the confusion only multiplies. We come from a culture where arranged marriages are still very much a thing, and falling in love before the age of 25 is often treated as some sort of rebellion. Try explaining to your parents that you want to date someone seriously in college. Their reaction is likely going to be, "But beta, what about your studies?" And I get it— they want the best for you—but at the same time, they don't understand that learning to love and be loved is just as important as learning calculus or memorizing historical dates. Relationships are part of growing up, and they help you understand who you are in ways that no textbook ever can.

However, in this fast-paced college environment, you're faced with people who are either commitment-phobic or those who think that dating means merging lives on day one. There's no in-between. On one hand, you've got people who'd rather write 3,000-word essays than commit to a second date, and on the other hand, you've got people planning wedding invitations after one shared meal at the campus canteen. It's a circus out there, and most of us are just trying to figure out which ring we belong in.

Adding to the confusion is social media, which makes every single relationship look like it's straight out of a Bollywood movie. Perfect couple selfies, vacation pictures, and surprise gifts—all designed to make you feel like you're failing at the relationship game if you're not living up to these Instagram able standards. But, let's be real: those relationships often have more filters than actual depth. It's like everyone is chasing this idea of perfection rather than focusing on real, messy, flawed human connections.

So, yeah, falling in love or even trying to be in a relationship in college is hard—because everything around you are built for short-term thrills, and when you try to go against the current, you feel like you're the weird one. You start to wonder if maybe you're asking for too much when all you really want is someone who will actually text back and maybe hold your hand in public without making it seem like a contractual obligation. But hey, we live, we learn, and if nothing else, we'll have some hilarious stories to tell about our college dating lives when we're older. At the very least, we'll know how to spot a red flag from a mile away,

Generation lost?

Deeper connections are something that seem almost lost on today's generation, and it's a real shame. In a world where everything is instant, from food delivery to same-day shipping, we've come to expect the same speed and convenience from relationships. But here is the thing: meaningful connections take time. They require patience, understanding, and effort, all things that don't come with the swipe of a finger. For many of us in college, making a deeper connection feels like an alien concept. We're told by society, pop culture, and even our peers that it's better to keep things casual, keep things fun, and avoid emotional entanglements. But there's something so rewarding about taking the time to really get to know someone, beyond the surface-level stuff.

The truth is, human beings are wired for connection. We crave it, whether we admit it or not. Think about it—how many times have you felt lonely, even when you were surrounded by people? That's because surface-level interactions can't fulfill the need for deep, meaningful bonds. Sure, it's fun to go out with friends, have a few laughs, and party till 3 AM, but at the end of the day, it is the deeper connections that actually sustain us. These are the relationships where you can talk about your fears, your dreams, and your insecurities without feeling judged. The ones where you don't have to put up a front or pretend to be someone, you're not just to impress the other person.

In today's generation, where superficiality often trumps substance, we forget how vital it is to have relationships that go beyond temporary fun. Deeper connections aren't just for romance either—they're essential in friendships, too. We're constantly distracted by the idea of having lots of "friends" on social media, but how many of those people would actually be there for you in a crisis? How many truly understand who you are at your core? Making real connections means being vulnerable, which is scary, but it's also where the magic happens. It's where you find people who get you, who understand your weird quirks, and who will stand by you even when things get tough.

And let's face it—college life can be tough.

Sure, we can pretend we don't need anyone, but at some point, we all hit a wall. It could be stress from exams, homesickness, or feeling lost about the future. That's when those deep connections become invaluable. It is easy to get caught up in the fast-paced world of quick dating and fleeting friendships, but those are the times when you realize how hollow that kind of connection can be. When you're stressed and feeling down, the person who was only interested in casual fun isn't going to be the one who checks in on you. The friend who only hits you up for weekend plans isn't the one who'll be there when you need someone to talk to at 2 AM. These are the moments when you realize the importance of meaningful relationships.

At the end of the day, deeper connections aren't just about having someone to share your highs and lows with. They're about personal growth. When you're in a meaningful relationship, whether it's with a friend or a romantic partner, you learn so much about yourself. You learn how to communicate better, how to compromise, and how to truly understand another person's perspective. These are skills that will benefit you far beyond college life. In today's generation, where everything seems so fleeting, taking the time to nurture these connections might just be the key to finding a bit of stability and meaning in an otherwise chaotic world.

So, while short-term fun has its place, don't overlook the importance of deeper connections. Because at the end of the day, those are the relationships that will truly stand the test of time. And let's be honest—when you're old and gray, you're not going to look back and think, "Wow, I'm so glad I had 50 matches on Bumble in college." You're going to think about the people who really knew you, the ones who made a difference in your life, and the connections that helped you become who you are.

I URGE YOU TO "FALL IN LOVE"

Let's get one thing straight: being in your twenties is a weird, weird time. It's like everyone handed you a box of mismatched Lego pieces and said, "Build your life now!" Some people build skyscrapers, others construct an odd, wobbly hut, and then there's the rest of us who are just staring at the pieces wondering if a nap might be a better option. But here's something I've learned—falling in love in your twenties is one of the greatest, most chaotic things you can do for yourself. Love will teach you things that the so-called culture of short-term flings simply cannot. Short-term thrills sound fun and some might argue that a crucial part of being independent is having many casual flings without commitments. Yes, I know how dumb that logic sounds.

Look, there's a reason why they call it the "no commitment culture". Because much like actual culture, it's filled with rituals, customs, and rules that no one really understands. There's the DM slide, the cryptic texts at 1 a.m. that say, "u up?", and the ever-popular disappearing act when someone ghosts you super hard. Short-term fun has become like that trendy pop-up restaurant everyone is obsessed with. Everyone's eager to try it out, talk about how unique it is, post it on Instagram, and then, after a while, realize that all it served was a garnish of confusion with a side of vague emptiness.

Here's the truth: hookups are easy. They require little effort, minimal vulnerability, and usually less than ten minutes on Tinder. But what do they leave you with in the end? Often, just an awkward small talk the next morning? Does it dig into who you are or challenge you in ways that leave you better.?

On the other hand, falling in love—real love—is anything but easy, but that's precisely what makes it so rewarding. Falling in love is like agreeing to co-sign a lease for an apartment in a strange new world. You walk in with bright-eyed enthusiasm, and then you realize that love is not just romantic sunsets and filtered pictures; it's also someone stealing the blankets at 3 a.m. and the eternal debate over whether you actually listen when she is talking or just nodding.

Love is where you learn that people are more complicated than they look in their curated social media photos. It's where you learn patience, compassion, and even how to share your personal space without holding a grudge. In love, you must be brave enough to show someone the parts of you that are messy, scarred, and sometimes downright irritating—and they do the same. It's like showing someone all the skeletons in your closet and hoping they don't run for the hills.

And the lessons you take away? They aren't superficial, surface-level. In a real relationship, you learn that it's not just about what you can get from someone—it's about what you can give and what you're willing to share. Love shows you that you are more capable of generosity and understanding than you imagined, and that your patience sometimes has surprising depths.

Here's an inconvenient truth: love isn't always about the other person. Often, it becomes a mirror. In a good, healthy relationship, your partner will gently show you all the places you need to grow. And, spoiler alert, that usually involves a lot of uncomfortable self-reflection. Love is when someone says, "Hey, maybe the way you shut down in every argument isn't healthy," and instead of deflecting, you actually sit down with yourself and start unpacking why. No commitment culture won't do that for you. It will hand you a shiny night of fleeting fun but nothing that truly shapes your character. Plus, relationships test your ability to compromise and communicate. Not the classic, "Sure, we can watch your show tonight" kind of compromise, but the "Okay, let's actually talk about why I feel weird about this" kind. It forces you to use your words—to articulate feelings beyond the vague, "It's chill," which we've all overused when things are anything but chill. Love requires you to be specific, honest, and vulnerable, even when it feels like exposing yourself during a winter windstorm.

Falling in love in your twenties isn't about finding your "forever person" by the time you're thirty. It's not about following a prescribed timeline that society conveniently decided is ideal. It's about allowing yourself to experience a deeper kind of human connection. It's about learning who you are in the context of someone else, about growing into the kind of person who can genuinely give love, not just receive it. And let me tell you, there's nothing wrong with trying this so-called culture. But, at some point, you might wake up and realize that fleeting intimacy doesn't compare to someone who's willing to stick around for more than a season. You'll miss the small things that come from being genuinely known by someone—the inside jokes, the comfort of not needing to put on a show, the feeling of just being understood.

So, I urge you—fall in love. Fall messily, imperfectly, and authentically in love. Get hurt if you must, because pain is part of what makes us. If you're avoiding relationships because you're afraid of getting hurt, then newsflash—you're already hurting. You're missing out on the part of life that makes the colors just a little brighter and the winters a little warmer.

Relationships teach you that it's okay to let someone in, to share the space in your mind that nobody else gets to visit. You learn to love someone's quirks and flaws, and you find yourself wishing the best for them, even when you're no longer in their life. That kind of growth? That's the stuff that adds depth to your character, that makes you kinder and more resilient.

So, let's stop glorifying the short-term culture as the be-all and end-all of young adulthood. Hookups will give you stories, but relationships will give you depth. They'll leave marks on your soul—yes, sometimes scratches, but often beautiful, lasting impressions that shape the way you see the world. And isn't that what this whole bizarre, twenty-something experience is all about? Learning, feeling deeply, and adding meaning to all the chaos.

Fall in love. Fall hard. Get messy. Grow. Because if you think about it, life's too short to keep all your feelings in neat little boxes that never get opened. Sometimes, you need to just dive into the deep end, ready to learn to swim—even if you've only ever waded in the shallows.

Raising Above: Finding True Connections that Matter

In a world brimming with constant communication and shallow interactions, discovering genuine connections that resonate deeply with our values and aspirations can feel elusive. True connections, those that uplift, support, and inspire us, are not mere accidents. Rather, they are often the result of an intentional mindset and, for some, a belief in destiny. This balance between mindset and destiny plays a crucial role in shaping the quality of our relationships and determining whether we seize the opportunity to connect with the right people—or let them pass us by.

Understanding What True Connections" Really Mean

True connections are not simply about knowing someone or sharing mutual interests; they are about depth, authenticity, and alignment. Such relationships transcend the superficial and become sources of personal growth, emotional fulfilment, and intellectual stimulation. Whether they take the form of friendships, romantic relationships, or professional partnerships, true connections are distinguished by:

Authenticity - There is a genuine effort to understand and be understood. Both parties are honest about their values, aspirations, and flaws.

Mutual Support - These relationships provide emotional and mental support during challenging times, and celebrate success together.

Growth - True connections encourage personal and collective development. They challenge stagnation, urging individuals to improve.

While it is possible to form connections with many people, true connections are rare and precious. The challenge, therefore, lies in recognizing them when they present themselves and nurturing them.

Mindset: The Key to Recognizing True Connections

Our mindset shapes how we perceive the world, the people around us, and the connections we make. With the right mindset, we can open ourselves to forming genuine bonds by being more aware of how we interact with others and what we seek from relationships.

1. Openness and Vulnerability

A mindset that fosters true connections requires vulnerability. Many people avoid deep relationships because they fear rejection, judgment, or disappointment. However, without openness, it is difficult to develop authentic bonds. Embracing vulnerability means being honest about who we are and what we seek in relationships, even if it means exposing ourselves to potential hurt.

- Be willing to share personal stories, struggles, and dreams.

- Show empathy and listen actively to understand the other person's experiences.

This creates a foundation of trust, allowing the relationship to grow beyond surface-level interaction.

2. Intentionality in Relationships

Mindset also involves being intentional about whom we choose to connect with. True connections do not happen by chance; they are often cultivated through deliberate effort. Rather than waiting for the "right" people to come into our lives, we can actively seek relationships that align with our values and goals. This means:

- Engaging with communities and individuals who share similar passions or aspirations.

- Setting clear boundaries in relationships that do not serve personal growth.

- Fostering mutual respect and understanding in every interaction.

The more intentional we are in choosing relationships, the more likely we are to connect with people who enrich our lives and resonate with our core values.

3. Growth-Oriented Thinking

Relationships, especially true connections, require a mindset of growth and evolution. People evolve, and so do relationships. Holding on to outdated expectations or resisting change can hinder the development of deeper connections. Growth-oriented thinking involves:

- Recognizing that both parties in a relationship will change over time.

- Embracing those changes and adapting to the evolving dynamics of the connection.

- Encouraging personal growth in ourselves and others, seeing the relationship as a tool for mutual development rather than mere companionship.

4. Understanding Compatibility Beyond Surface Level

A growth mindset also helps us discern between superficial compatibility and deeper alignment. Often, we are drawn to people based on shared hobbies or common backgrounds. However, true connections stem from a more profound compatibility that goes beyond external factors. These relationships are based on shared values, long-term goals, and a vision for the future.

By prioritizing these deeper qualities, we increase the likelihood of forming lasting and meaningful connections.

Destiny: Are We Meant to Meet the Right People?

The idea that we are destined to meet certain people at specific points in our lives has been a topic of fascination for centuries. Whether we call it fate, destiny, or divine intervention, there is a common belief that the people who cross our paths do so for a reason. But are we really meant to meet the right people, or is it all just coincidence? As humans, we often seek meaning in the connections we form, especially when they have a significant impact on our lives. The concept of destiny offers a comforting narrative—that everything happens for a reason, and that the people who come into our lives are meant to shape us in ways we may not immediately understand.

On one hand, destiny could be seen as a grand, cosmic plan where certain individuals are meant to play pivotal roles in our personal journeys. Think about the people who've had a profound influence on you—a mentor, a close friend, or even a romantic partner. In hindsight, it often feels as if you were "meant" to meet them. These encounters, whether random or deliberate, sometimes feel too perfect to be mere coincidence. We might meet someone during a moment of crisis, and they help us in ways that completely transform our perspective. The timing, the circumstances, and the chemistry all align, making it seem like the universe had a hand in orchestrating the meeting.

Consider those moments when you meet someone and instantly click, as if you've known them for ages. These "right" people often enter our lives at crucial moments, when we're struggling with something or need guidance, companionship, or love. Some argue that these encounters are destiny's way of ensuring we don't go through life alone—that we have allies and teachers to help us grow, learn, and evolve. The idea is that these people were always meant to be part of our story, and that their presence is part of a larger, predetermined path.

However, the concept of destiny doesn't mean that every person who enters your life will stay. Sometimes, people are meant to teach us temporary lessons, even though difficult or painful experiences. Not all "right" people are there for a lifetime; some may appear just for a season, leaving a lasting impact before moving on. In this sense, destiny can be seen not as a guarantee of permanent bonds, but as a series of encounters meant to help us become the best versions of ourselves.

On the other hand, skeptics argue that life is random, and it's our own actions, choices, and coincidences that lead us to meet certain people, not some predetermined cosmic plan. In their view, the "right" people we meet are simply a result of shared interests, proximity, and timing. What we perceive as destiny is actually our brain finding patterns in randomness. In other words, we give meaning to these encounters after they happen, attributing a sense of purpose to what might just be chance.

But even if destiny plays a role, our choices matter just as much. Meeting the right people is one thing, but the effort we put into nurturing those relationships and how we choose to engage with them is equally important. Perhaps destiny lays the groundwork, but it's up to us to do something with the connections we are given. Whether or not we're "meant" to meet certain people, the real magic lies in what we do once we meet them.

In the end, whether you believe in destiny or not, there's no denying that the people who come into our lives shape us in profound ways. These connections help define who we are, and whether it's fate or coincidence, meeting the right people at the right time often feels like a small miracle, reminding us that human connection is one of the most powerful forces in life.

If the Other Person Doesn't Love You the Way You Want, It Doesn't Mean They Don't Love You

Love is one of the most profound emotions we experience as human beings. It can bring joy, fulfilment, and a sense of connection like no other feeling. However, love is also deeply complex. Often, we enter relationships with certain expectations about how love should be expressed and received. When our partner doesn't meet these expectations, It is easy to feel unappreciated or unloved. But love is not a one-size-fits-all emotion, and the way someone expresses love may differ greatly from what we imagine or desire. Just because someone doesn't love you in the way you want doesn't mean they don't love you.

Love Languages and Individual Differences

One of the most important aspects of understanding how love is expressed lies in the concept of *love languages*. Developed by Dr. Gary Chapman, the five love languages describe the different ways in which individuals give and receive love. They are:

- Words of affirmation

- Acts of service

- Receiving gifts

- Quality time

- Physical touch

Each person tends to have one or two dominant love languages that define how they show affection. For example, if someone's love language is acts of service, they may express love by doing helpful things for their partner, such as cooking a meal or fixing something around the house. However, if their partner's love language is words of affirmation, they may feel unloved because they expect verbal expressions like compliments or verbal reassurances.

In this situation, the partner who is providing acts of service is showing love, but their partner may not recognize it as such. Understanding love languages can greatly help bridge the gap between differing expressions of love, making it clear that just because someone loves differently, it doesn't mean they don't love at all.

Unmet Expectations in Relationships

When we enter a romantic relationship, many of us come with expectations that are shaped by past experiences, cultural influences, or societal norms. These expectations can be about how love should feel, look, or manifest in daily interactions. However, when reality doesn't align with these idealized visions, we may feel disappointed or start questioning the depth of our partner's affection.

For instance, if someone grows up watching romantic films where grand gestures and constant praise are the norm, they might expect their partner to express love in the same way. But in real-life relationships, love often shows up in more subtle, everyday actions—helping with chores, listening after a long day, or simply being present. The gap between expectation and reality can sometimes lead to frustration or feelings of neglect.

In these cases, It is important to reassess the situation and consider whether your partner's actions might still reflect love, just not in the manner you envisioned. People are individuals with different backgrounds, personalities, and ways of expressing emotions. What one person sees as romantic may not be the same for another, but that doesn't diminish the sincerity of the feeling.

A key factor in navigating differences in how love is expressed is communication. Open and honest conversations about needs, desires, and feelings can help partners understand each other better. Miscommunication is one of the most common reasons why someone may feel unloved in a relationship. If one partner is doing their best to show affection in their own way but the other partner doesn't recognize it, a conversation about what each person needs could be eye-opening.

For example, if one partner values quality time but feels their significant other isn't providing it, they should express this need clearly rather than harboring resentment. Conversely, the other partner may be more action-oriented, believing they are showing love through deeds rather than time spent together. Once both sides are aware of their differing approaches, they can compromise and make a conscious effort to meet in the middle.

Communication is also essential because it helps partners understand each other's vulnerabilities and past experiences, which often shape how they love. Some people may struggle with expressing affection openly because of their upbringing or past relationships, but this doesn't mean they are incapable of love. A patient and understanding partner who encourages dialogue can help uncover these layers.

Love is Not Conditional

It is also vital to understand that true love isn't conditional on meeting specific requirements or expectations. One of the greatest misunderstandings in relationships is thinking that love is only valid if it meets particular conditions. Real love allows for imperfections and differences. When you love someone, you accept that they may not always act or respond in the ways you desire, but this doesn't lessen the sincerity of their feelings.

Love grows when both partners acknowledge that it may take different forms and expressions. Expecting someone to love you in only one specific way can be limiting and may prevent the relationship from flourishing. If you hold tightly to your version of love, you might miss out on the unique ways your partner is showing their affection. Embracing these differences allows love to develop more organically and deeply.

Love is not static. Relationships evolve, and so do the ways partners express their affection. Patience is an important factor when it comes to love, as understanding how someone loves takes time. The beginning of a relationship is often filled with excitement and intense emotions, but as the relationship matures, love can deepen in ways that aren't always immediately obvious.

Growth in love requires both individuals to adapt and learn more about each other as time goes on. Sometimes, a partner might not initially understand how to show love in a way that resonates with you, but with time and communication, they can grow into that understanding. Love doesn't have to be perfect to be genuine. It is about being open to the journey and allowing both yourself and your partner room to grow together.

In the end, the way someone loves may not always match our idealized visions or expectations, but that doesn't mean their love is any less real or meaningful. Love is as diverse as the individuals who experience it, and no two people will express it in exactly the same way. Recognizing the different love languages, communicating effectively, and practicing patience are crucial to maintaining a healthy, loving relationship.

When we understand that love doesn't have to conform to a singular ideal, we open ourselves up to deeper connections and more fulfilling relationships. So, just because someone doesn't love you the way you want, it doesn't mean they don't love you. It just means their love speaks a different language, and with effort, It is a language that can be understood.

White Lies – The Beginning of Mistrust

In every relationship, trust forms the cornerstone. Whether it's between friends, family members, or romantic partners, trust is essential for building strong, lasting connections. Yet, trust isn't something that forms overnight. It grows over time, nurtured by honesty, consistency, and a sense of security. However, all of that can begin to unravel with something as seemingly harmless as a white lie.

A white lie, often viewed as a small, trivial falsehood, is typically told with good intentions. Perhaps it's to avoid hurting someone's feelings, to dodge an awkward conversation, or to smooth over a minor issue. For example, telling a friend that their haircut looks great when it doesn't or assuring your partner that everything is fine when you're actually upset. The lie feels benign, a way to maintain peace in the relationship. After all, it's just a small fib, right? But what happens when these small lies accumulate, when they start to chip away at the foundation of trust?

The Nature of White Lies

White lies are often justified as necessary evils. They are told to protect someone's feelings or to avoid unnecessary drama. In fact, many people might argue that telling the truth in every situation could lead to more harm than good. A spouse might fib about liking a meal their partner cooked, or a parent might tell a small lie to shield their child from disappointment. These instances seem innocent enough, and often, they are. But the problem with white lies not in their size or frequency but in the subtle shift they create in the dynamics of trust within a relationship.

When people start telling white lies, they are often motivated by the desire to preserve the harmony of the relationship. The intention is rarely malicious. However, as benign as they may seem, white lies introduce a form of deception. And deception, no matter how small, is a slippery slope. Over time, a pattern of dishonesty can begin to form, leading one or both parties to question the other's sincerity. The question then becomes: if they lied about something small, what else might they be hiding?

The Erosion of Trust

The impact of white lies on a relationship isn't always immediate. In fact, it's the gradual, cumulative effect of repeated small deceptions that can be most damaging. Trust in a relationship function like a bank account—every act of honesty deposits trust, and every lie, no matter how small, is a withdrawal. Eventually, a relationship can find itself in a deficit if the lies start to outweigh the honesty.

Take, for instance, a romantic relationship. A partner might tell a white lie to avoid conflict, like saying they're not upset about a missed date when, in reality, they're hurt. In the short term, the lie smooths things over, avoiding an argument or uncomfortable conversation. But over time, these unspoken truths begin to accumulate. The person who was lied to may begin to sense that things aren't as transparent as they seem. They might feel uneasy, unsure of what is real and what is being concealed. Gradually, suspicion creeps in, eroding the trust that once served as the bedrock of the relationship. Once trust begins to weaken, it can lead to a domino effect of mistrust. The person who senses dishonesty might start questioning more aspects of the relationship, even if the initial white lies were minor. What started as a small, seemingly harmless fib now casts a shadow over the entire relationship.

The Emotional Toll

One of the most significant effects of white lies is the emotional toll they take on both the person telling the lie and the one being lied to. For the person telling the lie, there's often a sense of guilt or discomfort. They may rationalize their behaviour by reminding themselves that they're doing it to protect their partner or avoid hurting their feelings, but deep down, the act of deception weighs on them. With each new lie, they may feel further distanced from their partner, as the growing need to maintain the facade creates emotional separation.

On the other hand, the person being lied to may begin to feel unsettled, even if they can't put their finger on why. Subconsciously, they might sense that something is off, that the connection doesn't feel as genuine or open as it once did. Over time, this can lead to feelings of insecurity, anxiety, and even resentment. The emotional distance created by white lies can result in misunderstandings, miscommunication, and eventually a breakdown in the relationship's emotional intimacy.

In a friendship, this could manifest as one friend avoiding difficult conversations, choosing instead to say what they think the other person wants to hear. While it may seem like a way to keep the peace, it ultimately fosters a lack of authenticity. The friend who senses dishonesty might start to withdraw, feeling as though they can't rely on their friend to be truthful or direct with them. This subtle distance can strain the relationship, creating a rift that becomes harder to bridge over time.

The Slippery Slope to Larger Lies

One of the most dangerous aspects of white lies is that they can open the door to larger lies. It's often said that lying becomes easier the more you do it, and this is particularly true when it comes to white lies. What starts as a small untruth told with the best of intentions can pave the way for bigger lies, especially if the person telling the lie gets away with it.

In a romantic relationship, for example, a partner might start by telling a white lie about something insignificant, like how they spent their evening. But once that lie has been accepted, they might feel emboldened to lie about more substantial matters, such as their feelings about the relationship or even their actions. With each new lie, the stakes get higher, and the potential for harm grows exponentially.

Before long, the relationship might be built on a foundation of dishonesty. And while the initial white lies may have been told to preserve harmony, they ultimately have the opposite effect, creating an environment of mistrust and suspicion. The trust that once held the relationship together has been chipped away, leaving both parties feeling disconnected and unsure of one another.

Restoring Trust After White Lies

Rebuilding trust after it has been damaged by white lies can be a challenging process. It requires open communication, a willingness to be vulnerable, and a commitment to honesty, even when the truth is uncomfortable. The person who has been lied to needs reassurance that they can trust their partner or friend again, and the person who told the lies must be willing to take responsibility for their actions. In many cases, this process begins with a heartfelt conversation about the impact of the lies on the relationship. Both parties must be willing to listen, to express their feelings openly, and to work together to rebuild the trust that has been eroded. It's not an easy process, but with time, effort, and a renewed commitment to honesty, it is possible to repair the damage caused by white lies.

Growing Together in a Relationship: A Journey Without Losing Yourself

Relationships are among the most enriching experiences in life, providing support, love, and companionship. But while they can bring joy and growth, they can also blur the lines between two individuals, leading to a loss of personal identity. In a healthy relationship, it's essential to grow together while maintaining your individuality. No one should prioritize the relationship over their self-worth, values, and well-being. Rather, the relationship should be an extension of who you are, not your entire identity. This delicate balance is crucial for both the health of the relationship and personal fulfilment. In this essay, we will explore the importance of self-preservation in relationships, strategies to maintain your identity, and how to foster mutual growth without losing yourself.

The Importance of Self-Preservation in Relationships

When people first enter relationships, there's often an overwhelming urge to prioritize the other person's needs, often to the detriment of their own. This is especially true when one person becomes overly reliant on the approval or presence of their partner, leading to an imbalance where one partner's needs eclipse the other's. While prioritizing a loved one can be natural, it's dangerous when done at the expense of your identity.

Losing yourself in a relationship means compromising your values, beliefs, interests, or boundaries just to maintain harmony or please your partner. This sacrifice may seem trivial at first, but over time, it can result in a deep sense of dissatisfaction, resentment, or even emotional exhaustion. In the long run, a relationship built on compromise at the expense of one's identity is unsustainable.

Moreover, an individual's sense of self is foundational to their well-being. Your interests, goals, friendships, and passions shape who you are. Letting these aspects fade away can cause you to become overly dependent on your partner for validation and happiness. This dynamic leads to insecurity, as your emotional state becomes entirely tied to the state of the relationship. Self-preservation is therefore crucial to emotional health, allowing you to stay grounded and fulfilled, regardless of the relationship's trajectory.

Growing Together While Maintaining Individuality

A thriving relationship is one where both partners grow together, but also independently. Just as a tree requires roots (personal identity) to stay grounded and branches (shared growth) to flourish, a relationship thrives when each person is secure in who they are and capable of growing alongside their partner.

1. Understanding the Concept of "We" Without Losing "Me"

The ideal relationship embodies a "we" mentality—two people working together toward shared goals and values. However, it's critical to strike a balance between the "we" and the "me." Maintaining your identity within the "we" means nurturing your hobbies, friendships, and aspirations without guilt or hesitation.

For example, if you're passionate about a hobby, you shouldn't't feel compelled to give it up just because your partner doesn't share that interest. Similarly, maintaining friendships outside the relationship is key to keeping your social identity intact. Individual hobbies and relationships help broaden your world and keep your sense of self strong.

2. Communication is Key

The foundation of a relationship built on mutual respect and growth is clear, open communication. Partners should feel safe to express their needs, desires, and boundaries without fear of being judged or dismissed. Regular discussions about personal and shared goals, expectations, and emotional needs can help both partners understand each other better and create space for individuality.

Effective communication also involves respecting each other's boundaries. If one partner needs time for personal activities or introspection, it's essential that the other respects this without feeling threatened or neglected. This space fosters growth both individually and as a couple.

3. Priorities Self-Care

Self-care is not a selfish act; it's an essential component of maintaining a healthy relationship. It involves regularly checking in with yourself to ensure that your emotional, mental, and physical well-being are intact. Self-care might look like taking time for solo activities, reflecting on personal goals, or even seeking therapy to work on self-growth.

In a relationship, prioritizing self-care ensures that you're showing up as your best self. A well-balanced person is more capable of supporting and enriching their partner without draining themselves emotionally. This balance allows both individuals to grow and maintain their well-being.

Fostering Growth journey

Healthy relationships are dynamic—they evolve and grow over time. Both partners should continually strive for personal growth while also nurturing the relationship.

1. Support Each Other's Personal Goals

One of the most beautiful aspects of a relationship is having a partner who encourages you to pursue your dreams and ambitions. This mutual support is essential for long-term growth and fulfilment. Rather than feeling threatened by your partner's individual success or passion, you should embrace it and contribute to it.

Supporting each other's growth can look like encouraging your partner to pursue a new job opportunity, taking up a new hobby together, or allowing each other the freedom to travel or pursue educational endeavors. A relationship thrives when both individuals feel fulfilled not only in their shared experiences but also in their personal growth.

2. Create Shared Goals Without Sacrificing Individual Aspirations

It's equally important to set shared goals that you can work toward as a couple. Whether it's saving for a house, planning a trip, or starting a family, shared goals provide direction and purpose. However, these shared goals should not come at the cost of individual aspirations.

For example, one partner may have career aspirations that involve travel, while the other might want to pursue a long-term project at home. These goals should be discussed openly, allowing both partners to compromise and support each other. Flexibility in achieving personal and shared goals is crucial to maintaining harmony and growth.

3. Embrace Change Together

As people evolve, so do relationships. Growth often comes with change, whether that's in career shifts, personal interests, or emotional needs. Embracing these changes together, while maintaining a strong sense of self, allows the relationship to adapt and grow over time.

It's important to periodically assess the relationship and ensure that it's still aligned with both individuals' evolving identities and values. Adapting to change, rather than resisting it, ensures that the relationship remains fulfilling for both partners.

Escape Delusion: Valuing Your body, Mind and Soul

Independence is not synonymous with turning oneself into an open commodity, available to anyone and everyone without boundaries or discernment. To call these fleeting encounters independence is not only a misunderstanding of what it means to be free but a subtle act of self-betrayal. Many in their twenties are convincing themselves that being emotionally unattached and physically available is empowering. They wear their serial entanglements like a badge of honor, believing that a string of temporary partners is a sign of liberation. In truth, this glorified "freedom" has become a mask for fear—fear of vulnerability, fear of being known too deeply, and most disturbingly, a fear of truly valuing oneself enough to demand respect.

When a person continuously participates in these shallow connections, their sense of worth begins to erode. The idea that one can sleep around without emotions and stay "untouched" by it all is, at its core, an absurd fantasy. Each encounter, each half-hearted embrace, chips away at one's self-worth. They might say, "It's just fun. I don't want anything serious." But underneath the bravado is an aching emptiness—one that no amount of fleeting affection can ever truly fill.

We must face the truth that making oneself readily available to anyone who shows interest is not a display of independence—it is a display of desperation for validation. When you repeatedly offer your body without your heart, without a connection, you send a message to yourself: "I'm not worthy of anything deeper. I do not deserve someone who wants me for more than a night." This is not freedom; this is entrapment in a vicious cycle of self-neglect and degradation.

Respect for oneself starts with the boundaries we set. To allow just anyone into the most intimate aspects of our lives without considering the impact on our mental and emotional well-being is reckless. Independence should not be about how easily one can avoid love, commitment, or attachment. True independence is knowing your value so deeply that you choose who deserves to know you—body, mind, and soul. Independence is having the courage to say "no" to those who do not respect you and "yes" to the standards that honor who you are.

The culture of casual flings attempts to redefine self-worth into something cheap and accessible. It tells us that love is outdated, that intimacy can be fractured into physical transactions without emotional consequence, and that anyone unwilling to participate is either uptight or old-fashioned. But in truth, it's this cycle of casual encounters that is outdated—empty connections lacking the warmth, commitment, and true intimacy that every person inherently deserves.

There is strength in demanding more. There is bravery in saying, "I am not for everyone. I am not someone's temporary amusement, their placeholder until something better comes along." Real independence lies in having standards, in being discerning about who gets your time, your energy, and your affection. It is not about shutting people out but about inviting only those in who see your true value and who are willing to invest in something deeper. It is time to shed the delusion that sleeping around without a care in the world is the epitome of modern freedom. It is time to recognize that the greatest act of independence is to love oneself enough to refuse to be used, to refuse to be part of a cycle that reduces a person to mere moments of pleasure. Let independence be redefined—not as the ability to run from connection, but as the courage to build it with people worthy of our time and our hearts.

Respect Your Boundaries, and People Will Respect You

Respecting personal boundaries is essential for maintaining healthy relationships, fostering mutual respect, and preserving emotional well-being. Whether in friendships, family, or professional settings, boundaries are the invisible lines that define what is acceptable and comfortable for each individual. When you respect your own boundaries, you project a sense of self-worth, and others are more likely to respect you in return. This concept forms the foundation of personal empowerment and social harmony.

Understanding Boundaries

Boundaries are the limits you set regarding what you will or will not accept in various areas of your life. These can be physical, emotional, or psychological. For example:

- Physical boundaries include personal space and physical touch. Some people may feel comfortable with hugs, while others prefer handshakes.

- Emotional boundaries involve protecting your feelings and emotional state. This could mean not allowing others to speak to you in a derogatory manner or dismiss your emotions.

- Psychological boundaries focus on your mental state, including the types of conversations or behaviors you will tolerate. For instance, you may not wish to engage in gossip or be involved in discussions that drain your energy.

Understanding your own limits helps you identify where your boundaries lie, which is the first step toward asserting them.

The Importance of Self-Respect

Respecting your boundaries starts with self-respect. If you don't honor your own needs and limits, it's difficult to expect others to do so. Self-respect involves acknowledging your worth and recognizing that you deserve to be treated with dignity. When you consistently allow people to overstep your boundaries, you send a message that you do not value yourself, which can lead to mistreatment or exploitation.

Establishing and maintaining boundaries requires self-awareness. Reflect on what makes you uncomfortable or stressed in different relationships and scenarios. Once you've identified these triggers, it becomes easier to communicate your boundaries clearly to others. Setting boundaries isn't about pushing people away; it's about creating a safe space for yourself.

How Respecting Boundaries Affects Relationships

When you set and respect your own boundaries, it teaches others how to treat you. People tend to mirror the behavior you exhibit, so when you project confidence and self-respect, they are more likely to respect your space and needs. Clear boundaries can also help prevent misunderstandings and conflicts in relationships.

For instance, in a work environment, if you establish that you do not respond to work-related messages after hours, this boundary protects your personal time. When consistently upheld, it sets a standard for colleagues to respect your downtime.

In personal relationships, boundary-setting ensures mutual respect. Healthy relationships thrive on trust, communication, and respect for each other's limits. If someone cares about you, they will honor your boundaries without seeing them as a threat. On the other hand, people who repeatedly disrespect your boundaries may not have your best interests at heart, and it's crucial to reassess those relationships. While it is important to set boundaries, it is equally important to be flexible when appropriate. Rigid boundaries can sometimes isolate you from others or create unnecessary friction. The key is to be assertive about your non-negotiable while maintaining open communication.

Being flexible with boundaries does not mean compromising your values or allowing disrespect. It simply means recognizing when a situation may require a bit of give-and-take for the sake of maintaining a relationship or achieving a common goal. Balance is key.

Respecting your boundaries creates a ripple effect that positively impacts all areas of your life. When people respect you, they are more likely to treat you with kindness, fairness, and consideration. Furthermore, respecting others' boundaries strengthens your relationships, as it builds trust and mutual understanding. In a world where boundaries are respected, individuals feel safer, more valued, and more connected.

Ultimately, respecting your boundaries and the boundaries of others leads to stronger, more respectful, and healthier relationships. By prioritizing your needs and limits, you set the standard for how you expect to be treated, and this fosters an environment of mutual respect.

Beyond the Surface – Cultivating Depth in Relationships

In a world where surface-level interactions often define relationships, many couples find themselves stuck in routines or focusing on superficial aspects of their partnership. It is easy to get caught up in the day-to-day concerns of work, household chores, or appearances, but the true magic of a lasting and meaningful connection requires delving beyond these distractions.

To push the boundaries of your relationship and foster a deeper understanding with your partner, consider the following strategies:

1. Priorities Emotional Vulnerability

One of the most significant barriers to deeper understanding is the fear of being vulnerable. Many couples hesitate to share their true thoughts, feelings, or fears, worrying that it may create conflict or make them appear weak. However, vulnerability is not a weakness—it is a doorway to emotional intimacy.

Be Honest About Your Feelings: Speak openly about what excites, scares, or bothers you without the filter of trying to "protect" your partner from the truth. Authentic conversations about your inner world allow both partners to understand each other beyond their surface personalities.

Practice Active Listening: When your partner opens up, make sure to listen without judgment or the need to offer immediate solutions. Creating space for your partner to express their emotions fosters trust, as they will feel safe in sharing their thoughts with you.

2. Move Past Routine Conversations

Couples often get trapped in mundane conversations about daily tasks—what to eat, who will handle chores, or what's on the calendar for the week. These necessary discussions are part of life but should not define the entire relationship.

- Ask Deeper Questions: Instead of sticking to logistical conversations, ask your partner about their dreams, aspirations, or personal struggles. Dive into their views on life, love, and even existential topics. For example, ask, *"What's something you've never told anyone but wish you could?" or "What does love mean to you now, versus when we first met?"

- Reflect on Growth Together: Take time to revisit how far you've come as a couple. Reflecting on your shared experiences and challenges helps you see the depth and complexity of your relationship. Celebrate not only the milestones but also the personal growth both of you have experienced.

3. Cultivate Shared Experiences That Encourage Growth

Superficiality often thrives when couples only engage in comfortable, repetitive activities. To move past this, it's essential to challenge yourselves to grow individually and together. Engaging in new experiences that push your boundaries can strengthen your bond.

Take on Challenges Together: This could be learning a new skill, tackling a shared goal, or even confronting personal fears as a team. Whether it's traveling to unfamiliar places, working on a creative project, or supporting each other in personal growth, facing challenges side-by-side forces you both to rely on each other in deeper ways.

Practice Mindful Presence: Being present in the moment is key to creating a deep connection. Engage in activities that force you to be fully aware of each other—this could be anything from taking long walks without distractions to practicing mindful communication exercises like eye-gazing or even meditation.

4. Develop Emotional Intelligence Together

Emotional intelligence is the ability to understand, manage, and navigate your own emotions and those of others. It's one of the most crucial elements of a healthy, deep relationship. By working on emotional intelligence together, couples can communicate more effectively and handle conflicts with greater empathy.

Learn Each Other's Emotional Triggers: Take the time to understand what triggers negative emotions in your partner and why. These insights will help you respond with compassion instead of reacting with frustration during difficult moments.

Practice Self-Awareness: Encourage each other to regularly reflect on your own emotional states and how they impact the relationship. Self-awareness fosters accountability and prevents misunderstandings from turning into deep-rooted resentments.

5. Build a Foundation of Trust and Intimacy

True intimacy goes far beyond physical connection—it's about trust, shared vulnerability, and mutual respect. By cultivating a strong foundation of trust, you create the space for both partners to grow into their most authentic selves.

Be Consistent in Your Actions: Trust is built through consistent, reliable behavior over time. Show your partner that you are someone they can rely on not just in the big moments but also in the small, everyday instances.

Nurture Physical and Emotional Intimacy: Physical closeness is important, but emotional intimacy is equally vital. Take time for physical affection, but also spend quality time simply talking, laughing, and being present with each other without distractions.

6. Embrace Conflict as an Opportunity for Growth

It's easy to view conflict as something to avoid or minimize, but disagreements, when approached with love and empathy, can be powerful moments for growth. Superficial relationships often crumble under the pressure of conflict because the partners haven't learned how to navigate it healthily.

Shift Your Perspective on Conflict: Instead of seeing arguments as destructive, view them as opportunities to understand each other better. Often, conflicts reveal hidden needs or unresolved feelings. By addressing these deeper issues, you strengthen your bond.

Use "I" Statements: During conflicts, focus on expressing your feelings rather than blaming your partner. Statements like, "I feel hurt when..." instead of "You always..." keep the conversation from becoming accusatory and help both partners communicate their needs more effectively.

7. Explore Each Other's Inner Worlds.

At the core of every individual lies a rich, complex inner world that can only be understood through intentional exploration. In long-term relationships, people sometimes assume they already know everything about their partner, which can lead to disconnection.

Be Curious About him/her: Cultivate curiosity by regularly asking about your partner's thoughts, beliefs, and emotions. Even if you've been together for years, there are always new layers to uncover. Ask questions that reveal their inner world—what they're currently passionate about, what they're struggling with, or what they dream of achieving in the future.

Support Each Other's Growth: Encourage personal growth and individuality within the relationship. Being supportive of your partner's personal journey fosters respect and admiration, which are essential to deepening your bond.

Moving on is a Myth

They tell you to move on, as if love is a jacket, you can take off and hang up, just because the weather has changed. But the truth is, you don't move on from someone you truly cared for. You carry them with you—in the memories that glow like embers, in the lessons that settle quietly in your bones, and even in the scars that have shaped you into who you are now. Moving on isn't a line you cross; it's a myth we've spun, a neat idea to contain a deeply human mess.

The concept of moving on suggests there's a finish line, some destination where you emerge, miraculously free of the person you loved. But love doesn't work that way. When you share pieces of yourself with someone, those pieces don't simply come back like misplaced puzzle parts. You change, they change, and the love—no matter where it went—leaves fingerprints behind. Yet, none of this means that you should stop living or that the shadow of what was, should swallow what you can be. The trick isn't to try to forget or pretend that the love didn't matter. The goal is to acknowledge it fully, to let it carve its place in your story, and then to let yourself grow around it. You don't have to erase the love to make space for what's next. Instead, you take it, place it like a delicate keepsake on the shelf of your heart, and move forward—step by step, lesson by lesson.

There's a beauty in looking back at what once was and feeling the warmth that those moments gave you. The laughter on a lazy Sunday afternoon, the comfort of someone holding your hand in silence, those comfy movie dates, the adventures you never thought you'd have—these are the threads that stitched joy into your life. And why should you want to forget that?

The problem comes when people mistake moving on with forgetting. The love you shared was real, and its memories are just as valid. They deserve a smile, not a sigh, because they were moments that once painted your world in vibrant colors. Cherishing these memories doesn't mean you're stuck—it means you're wise enough to see the value in what you had, without letting it define your every step. It's okay to remember someone and feel that pang in your chest. It means you lived, you cared, you felt deeply. It's proof that you risked your heart and let someone in, and that's nothing short of courageous. But instead of letting the loss define you, use it to understand what you want, what you value, and what you're capable of giving and receiving. Growth isn't a rejection of the past; it's an acceptance of it, and a decision to let it shape you into something stronger, kinder, and wiser.

Moreover, this isn't about wallowing in self-blame or pointing fingers at what went wrong. It's about growing from the experience. It's about looking at your reflection, acknowledging the flaws and strengths, and deciding to be better—not for anyone else, but for you. The loss of a relationship can be like pruning a tree—it hurts, and it leaves you bare in parts, but ultimately, it gives you room to grow again, stronger and fuller than before. You don't have to force yourself to forget someone just to prove you've "moved on." What you can do is allow the pain to soften, to shape you, and to let it fuel your journey into becoming a better version of yourself. Growth isn't linear—it's not about sprinting to the finish line of "moving on" but about taking each day as it comes, letting the pain lose its sting a little at a time, and eventually finding joy in new moments.

So instead of obsessing over the idea of moving on—as if love is something that needs to be left behind—embrace the idea of moving through. You move through the memories, letting them teach you, letting them guide you, but never letting them anchor you. You move through the sadness until it's no longer heavy in your chest, until it's just a part of you—like a faint scar from a wound that has healed. And with every day, you add new chapters, new joys, new people, and new experiences that add depth and richness to your story.

Moving on, then, isn't about leaving love behind. It's about transforming it into something that pushes you forward, that makes you understand yourself better, and that helps you step into a new day with grace. Love isn't meant to be a weight; it's a force, and when it's time, you can let it propel you into the unknown, taking the lessons, the good, and even the hurt—because all of it matters. The next time someone tells you to "move on," take a breath and remember—you're allowed to move at your own pace. You're allowed to keep the memories close, to honor the love that shaped you. Let go of the pressure to forget and instead use the experience to learn, to reflect, and to grow.

Moving forward isn't about finding someone new to fill the gaps, nor is it about forgetting what once made you feel whole. It's about deciding that despite the love lost, despite the hurt endured, your story isn't over yet. You're still writing it, page by page, and each word is richer because of the journey you've been on. And maybe, just maybe, that's the real way we grow—by accepting that moving on is a myth, but moving forward, with all that we've gained, is very real.

Chapter 6
USING FREEDOM, THE RIGHT WAY

I know when I talk about freedom it's a sensitive topic, it's quite ironic of me to write a chapter about how you should use your freedom right? The whole reason behind having freedom is to do what in your mind without someone giving you any instructions. But just hear me out

Entering college feels like stepping into an entirely new universe. It's not just about moving to a different location, but it's a complete lifestyle shift. Suddenly, you're surrounded by unfamiliar faces, navigating through a maze of new experiences, and for some, even adapting to a different culture or country. It's an exhilarating time because, for the first time, you're tasting true freedom and independence.

Gone are the days of seeking permission from parents for every little outing or excursion. There's a distinct lack of constant supervision, and you realize that you're now in charge of yourself. Your decisions, your rules, your choices - they all shape your path, and there's no one else to credit or blame for the outcomes. It's a thrilling yet daunting realization that you're solely responsible for charting your course in this new phase of life.

Is this freedom empowering, exciting and long awaited yes to all three but only if you know how to use freedom the right way.

Using freedom responsibly means understanding that our actions have consequences. Sure, we can skip class or pull an all-nighter before an exam, but that's not exactly the smartest move, is it? It's about finding that balance between having fun and staying on top of our responsibilities.

But here's the cool part: when we use our freedom effectively, it can actually enhance our college experience. It's about making the most out of every opportunity that comes our way. Whether it's joining clubs, volunteering, or pursuing our passions, college is the perfect time to explore and grow as individuals.

So yeah, freedom in college is pretty awesome, but it's also a lesson in maturity. It's about making conscious choices that will ultimately shape our futures. And hey, isn't that what college is all about?

When I first set foot on campus, it was like a chicken finally breaking free from the coop. No more "beta, where are you going?" or "come home by 9 p.m. sharp." Just the sweet taste of freedom, like binging on that spicy biriyani plate you love without someone reminding you of the consequences later. But let me tell you, freedom is a double-edged sword—just like that spicy red chutney served alongside your mom's that tastes great until it burns your insides.

Freshman year was my first real taste of independence. No one to dictate when I should study or, more importantly, when to sleep. I could stay up all night binge-watching TV shows, hit snooze on morning alarms without guilt, and skip classes like they were optional—because, technically, they were! It felt like I was living in a Bollywood movie where the hero has no responsibilities, only songs and fun. But then reality hit me.

One semester, I got so carried away by this freedom that I almost forgot the main reason I was on campus—to get an education and make my parents proud (and avoid disappointing relatives who would never let me forget it). Instead of attending lectures, I was busy attending late-night chai sessions and impromptu road trips with friends. Assignments? Procrastinated till the last minute like a true procrastination champion. I thought I was living my best life, but in reality, I was digging myself into a pit deeper than any family WhatsApp group discussion.

Then came the moment of truth—my end-of-semester grades. Let's just say they weren't exactly the hero's triumphant moment in a Bollywood climax. They were more like that moment when the hero gets slapped by his father just like in Kabhi Khushi Kabhie Gham when Amitabh Bachchan's character, slaps his son Rahul, played by Shah Rukh Khan, when Rahul defies him by marrying a girl of his choice. (And the background music stops. I had wasted my freedom in the worst way possible. Instead of using all the resources and opportunities available to me, I had treated college like a vacation spot with free Wi-Fi.

It took a semester on academic probation and a long, hard look in the mirror (plus a guilt trip of a phone call from my parents) to realize that freedom isn't just about doing whatever you want. It's about learning to make decisions that won't come back to bite So, after a stern pep talk with myself, I decided to balance my freedom with responsibility. Sure, I still hang out with friends and enjoy the occasional midnight Maggi and bike rides, but now I actually study and show up to class on time (mostly).

In the end, college is like a masala-filled adventure: yes, there's fun, but it's also about preparing yourself for the real world. If you don't balance your freedom with a little self-discipline, you'll end up with more than just academic struggles—you might end up with your parents reminding you of it for the rest of your life!

Let's keep in short and outline this chapter into three Sets

After all its about Freedom let me just outline a few ways in which you can make the most of it and rest is on you, like I said your rules your choice just thinks of me as an invisible guide.

Strategies for Building Self-Discipline

1. Time Management Techniques

Mastering time management is like finding the cheat code for college. Creating a weekly schedule, using to-do lists, and breaking tasks into bite-sized pieces can work wonders. I swear by my planner—it's my lifeline! It helps me juggle lectures, study time, and still squeeze in a little Netflix. Remember, a well-planned day means less stress and more samosas later!

The 1-3-5 Rule: Each day, identify one big task, three medium tasks, and five small tasks to accomplish. This method simplifies your daily to-do list, making it feel more achievable and less overwhelming.

The ABCDE Method: This prioritization technique involves categorizing tasks into five groups:

- A: Must-do tasks (high priority)
- B: Should-do tasks (medium priority)
- C: Nice-to-do tasks (low priority)
- D: Delegate tasks where possible
- E: Eliminate unnecessary tasks. This method helps you focus on what truly matters.

2. Setting and Adhering to Deadlines

Deadlines are like the lifebuoys in a sea of assignments. They keep you afloat and help avoid that last-minute panic that usually results in a flurry of coffee cups and frantic typing. I set personal deadlines a few days ahead of the actual due dates—kind of like preparing for a festival a week in advance. It gives me a buffer for those unexpected life moments—like when your Wi-Fi decides to take a vacation right when you need it the most!

3. Creating Accountability Systems

Having accountability partners is like having a gym buddy but for studying. Whether it's joining study groups or simply sharing your goals with friends, accountability keeps you on track. Knowing that someone else is aware of your ambitions pushes you to follow through. Plus, using productivity apps is like having a personal trainer for your tasks—reminding you to stay focused when you'd rather scroll through memes.

4. Overcoming Procrastination

Procrastination is the arch-nemesis of every student, including me. It's so tempting to put off that assignment until the last minute. But I've found that breaking tasks into smaller chunks can help get the ball rolling. Instead of staring at a massive project, I tackle it piece by piece—like finishing a large plate of biryani, one bite at a time. Using the Pomodoro technique (25 minutes of work, 5 minutes of break) helps keep me focused and minimizes distractions. Plus, I remind myself of the not-so-glamorous consequences of procrastination—like late-night panic and a questionable internet history.

In conclusion, overcoming procrastination and building self-discipline isn't easy, but it's definitely achievable. With a sprinkle of planning, a dash of self-awareness, and maybe a little help from your friends (and a good chai), you can turn those chaotic college days into a smooth ride towards success!

Financial Freedom? Does that really exist in college?

Ah, college life – Maggi noodles, chai, and perpetual "brokeness". If there's one thing that unites us across all campuses, it's the universal experience of being financially challenged. Sure, you might spot the occasional rich kid who drives a shiny car and wears the latest fashion, but for the majority of us, financial struggles are as integral to college life as bunking lectures and last-minute exam cramming.

Let's face it, no one really talks about being broke in college. It's like this big, unspoken elephant in the room – only this elephant is wearing second-hand clothes and surviving on 20-rupee vada pavs. But why should we be ashamed? I say let's embrace our "kanjoos" (stingy) status with pride!

First off, there's the art of budget living. If you haven't mastered it yet, college will make you a pro in no time. Who needs Starbucks when you can get a cutting chai at the local tapri for a fraction of the cost? Sure, your Instagram might not be as glam, but who cares when you're saving enough money to buy that extra plate of momos?

And speaking of food, let's not forget the dining hall hacks. You learn to time your visit perfectly to avoid the soggy samosas and get the fresh batch instead. Plus, there's the bonus of making friends with the mess workers – a smile and a bit of small talk Can sometimes score you an extra rassgulla or an extra serving of

So why the stigma, I ask? Let's own our financial struggles. They build character, give us funny stories to tell, and most importantly, they teach us the true value of things. We might be broke, but we're rich in resourcefulness, friendships, and life skills.

After all, who needs loads of money when you have the kind of friends who share their maggi with you at 2 AM, who understand the joy of finding a hidden 100-rupee note in your old jeans, and who will laugh with you when you're reminiscing about the days when a luxury meant an extra cheese slice on your sandwich?

– may our wallets be light, but our hearts be full!

The Realistic College Budget: A Survival Guide

Welcome to College Financial Survival 101! Get ready, because we're about to dive into the crazy, chaotic, and often comical world of budgeting. Spoiler alert: it's not all samosas and chai... well, mostly.

Assessing Your Income

First things first: where's the money coming from? For most of us, it's a mix of pocket money from parents, part-time jobs, scholarships, and that random 500-rupee note you found in your old jeans.

Imagine the joy when you receive your first allowance for the month from home. You feel like Ambani for a day, splurging on fancy coffee and maybe even a nice dinner. But then reality kicks in, and suddenly, you have no idea how to cover for the months' rent, with your landlord sending daily reminders or to put it into better words threats to pay rent ASAP

Listing Your Expenses

Next, jot down all your expenses. This includes the obvious ones like semester fees, hostel fees, and food, but don't forget the sneaky costs like laundry, photocopying notes, and those midnight Maggi runs.

"Budgeting is a breeze," I thought. Then I remembered that laundry needs to happen more than once a month and how we foolishly underestimate how much we spend on Zomato and 10 min delivery apps like blinkit. Yes, we are a very lazy and "need everything right away" kind off spoiled now generation"

Now, match your income against your expenses. Allocate funds for each category, I remember My first budget was tighter than the traffic in Bangalore so leaves a little wiggle room for unexpected costs,

Pro tip: always overestimate your Zomato/Swiggy expenses They're like little black holes for your money. You never know when your money gets teleported from your Gpay account.

Using Budgeting Tools

Use budgeting apps like Walnut or Money View to track your spending. These apps can send you alerts when you're nearing your limits—kind of like a financial lifeguard preventing you from drowning in debt.

Walnut once alerted me that I'd spent 500 rupees on chai in a week. Five hundred! I guess my love for chai needs to be re-evaluated. Or maybe I should just admit my addiction and cut back elsewhere. Tough choices.

Cutting Costs

Find creative ways to cut costs. Use student discounts, buy used textbooks, cook at home, and share subscriptions. Every little bit helps.

We split a Netflix subscription among six hostel mates. Cue the chaos when we all tried to watch our favorite shows simultaneously on different devices. We couldn't due to the 2-device limit and then our hostel turned into a courtroom with each party arguing why they should me the one watching Netflix right now.

Saving and Emergency Funds

Set aside a bit of money each month for savings and emergencies. Trust me, the peace of mind is worth the sacrifice. Even if it's just a few hundred rupees, it can grow over time.

I started an emergency fund after a pani puri-related disaster. Turns out, binging on street food isn't sustainable (or cheap). Now, I stash away 500 rupees each month, just in case I need it for actual emergencies, like running out of data.

Sticking to Your Budget

Sticking to your budget is the hardest part. It requires discipline and sometimes saying no to fun plans. But remember, being broke is not fun either.

I once had to turn down a spontaneous road trip because it wasn't in the budget. Sure, it was a bummer, but I consoled myself with a Netflix binge (thanks to my parents' account). I like to think of it as a win for fiscal responsibility.

Budgeting in college isn't about depriving yourself; it's about making smart choices so you can enjoy your time without financial stress. Embrace the journey, laugh at the hiccups, and remember, even the best budgeters have off days.

Final Thought: If all else fails, there's always Maggie. It's the timeless hero of broke college students everywhere. Bon appétit!

Now let me share with you my secrets that I used throughout my college life—well, after my first year. I went broke several times and once started the month with around 20,000 rupees, only to blow it all by the 8th. These experiences taught me some sneaky habits to survive

Alright, future financial wizards, it's time to talk about saving. No, not saving the planet or saving the last slice of pizza—though both are noble causes. We're talking about saving money, one small step at a time.

1. The Power of Spare Change: The Old-School Piggy Bank

Yes, it's old school, but hear me out. Get yourself a jar, a piggy bank, or even an old coffee can. Toss in your spare change every day. Those nickels and dimes add up faster than you think.

Example: I started throwing my spare change into a jar labeled "Summer Break Fund." By the end of the semester, I had enough for a road trip with my buddies and still money left for some snacks for the road. Score!

2. Round-Up Savings: The Digital Piggy Bank

Use apps your bank's round-up feature to save without thinking. Every time you make a purchase, these apps round up to the nearest Hundredth value or whatever preset value you prefer and put the difference into a savings account or investment.

Example: I bought a coffee for 175, and the app rounded it up to 200 bucks, saving that extra 25 rupees. Over a month, those little bits add up. It's like a stealthy ninja savings plan.

4. Automate Your Savings: Set It and Forget It

Set up an automatic transfer from your checking to your savings account. Even if it's just 200 a week, it adds up over time without you having to lift a finger.

Example: I set up a 250 rupees weekly transfer to my savings account. At first, I barely noticed it, but after a semester, I had enough saved up for those unexpected "emergencies" (like when the cafeteria ran out of pizza and I had to order in).

5. Cash-Only Days: Go Old School Once a Week

Pick one day a week where you only use cash. It makes you more mindful of your spending because when the cash is gone, it's gone.

Example: I designated Fridays as cash-only days. It made me think twice about every purchase. Plus, watching my cash dwindle kept me from impulse-buying new FIFA game for my PlayStation

7. Free Entertainment: Fun Without the Funds

Explore free events on campus or in your community. Movie nights, free concerts, game nights—there are often plenty of options that don't cost a dime.

Example: We discovered that our university had free movie nights every Friday. Instead of hitting the expensive cinema, we grabbed some snacks and enjoyed the free flicks. More money for other things (like the popcorn fund).

8. The No-Spend Challenge: Test Your Willpower

Challenge yourself to a no-spend day or even a week. Only spend on essentials and see how much you can save.

Example: My friends and I did a no-spend weekend challenge. It turned into a fun adventure of finding free things to do, and I ended up saving more than I expected. Plus, it gave us some hilarious stories to tell.

9. Student Discounts: Flash That ID

Always ask about student discounts. You'd be surprised how many places offer them—restaurants, shops, movie theatres, and even software subscriptions.

Example: I flashed my student ID at a local bookstore and got 10% off. Another time I went out to a Italian restaurant that had special discounts for college goers for students week. It doesn't sound like much, but those small discounts add up, and I felt like a savvy spender.

The 24-Hour Rule

Before making a non-essential purchase, wait 24 hours. This helps curb impulse buying and often, the urge to buy will pass.

Example: I almost bought a fancy gaming laptop on a whim. After 24 hours, I realized my trusty old PlayStation works just fine for the rare times me and by mates sit together to play a couple of games and bash some buttons, Saved myself 4and a lot of buyer's remorse.

Chapter 7

WORDPLAY: MASTERING THE CHAT GAME
THE FILTER COFFEE TECHNIQUE

The Filter Coffee Technique: Brewing Better Communication

In the chaotic world of college life, effective communication is your secret ingredient for survival. Whether you're trying to clarify a group project (because let's be honest, half the group hasn't read the assignment), resolving a conflict over who gets to sit in the front row during lectures, or simply connecting with your friends, the way you communicate can either save the day or make it a total drama. So, let's dive into the Filter Coffee Technique—a method of communication as rich and satisfying as your favorite cup of filter coffee. Here's how to use it to enhance your interactions and maintain your mental peace (because we all need that!).

Brewing Patience: Taking Time to Formulate Responses

Just like filter coffee needs time to drip and develop its flavor (and we're not talking about that instant stuff!), good communication requires a bit of patience. When tempers flare, it's all too easy to jump in with a reaction that's as hasty as your morning cup of chai when you're late for class. Here's how to brew your thoughts effectively:

- **Pause and Reflect:** Before firing off a response (or a "That's not fair!"), take a moment to breathe. Channel your inner Zen master—this pause can save you from unnecessary chaos and allow you to respond thoughtfully. Plus, it'll give you time to consider whether that group member really deserves your wrath over the missing assignment.

- **Choose Your Words Wisely:** Think about the impact of your words. You want to sound clear and kind, not like the cranky uncle at a family wedding. Ask yourself, "Would I want to hear this?" If the answer is no, maybe rephrase!

- **Stay Focused on the Issue:** Avoid dragging up the time your friend borrowed your notes and never returned them. Keep it on track and work towards a solution.

Filtering Clarity: Ensuring Clear and Concise Communication

Filter coffee is known for its clarity (and the lack of mystery ingredients), so let your communication be just as clear. Clear communication can save everyone a lot of time and confusion—trust me, nobody wants to revisit the "What did we decide about the project?" conversation for the third time.

- **Be Specific and Direct:** Instead of saying, "You never help with group projects," try, "I feel stressed when I have to handle all the workload alone. Can we share the tasks more evenly?" Your friends might not be mind readers, but they can read the vibe if you say it right!

- **Use 'I' Statements:** Frame your thoughts from your perspective. Instead of saying, "You always ignore my suggestions," try, "I feel overlooked when my ideas aren't considered." It's like offering filter coffee instead of instant coffee; you get a better response!

- **Summaries and Confirm:** After discussing key points, sum it up. Phrases like, "So, we're all agreed on this?" can be lifesavers. It's like a final sip of coffee, confirming you've got the flavor just right.

Infusing Empathy: Adding Warmth and Understanding

The best filter coffee is brewed with care, just like your conversations should be infused with empathy and understanding. A little warmth can go a long way in building connections (and maybe saving you from that awkward silence in the group).

- **Listen Actively:** Show genuine interest in what the other person is saying. Nod like you're really into it (bonus points for maintaining eye contact!). Sometimes, people just want to know you're listening—and that's a lot easier than dealing with miscommunication.

- **Acknowledge Feelings:** Even if you don't agree, saying something like, "I get that you're frustrated" can work wonders. It's like adding sugar to your coffee—makes it easier to swallow!

- **Express Understanding:** Reflect back what you've heard. For example, "It sounds like you're worried about the deadline. Let's figure out a plan together." You'll be the hero of the group, and who doesn't want that?

Maintaining Consistency: Building Trust Over Time

Just as consistency in brewing filter coffee leads to a reliable taste, consistent communication builds trust. No one wants to be left guessing if you'll show up for the next group meeting—be the reliable friend we all need!

- **Regular Check-ins:** Especially with group projects, check in regularly. It's better than the last-minute panic that hits when you realize no one has done anything!

- **Follow Through on Promises:** If you said you'd handle the slides for the presentation, do it! Reliability fosters trust, and that is the true essence of teamwork.

- **Be Honest and Transparent:** Honesty is crucial. If you're struggling, it's better to communicate openly rather than pretending you're fine. It's like brewing coffee; sometimes, you just need to admit when you need a little extra help.

Adapting the Brew: Customizing Communication for Different Situations

Just like you might adjust your coffee brew for different occasions (yes, we all have that one friend who prefers her coffee with an extra shot of drama), adapt your communication style based on context.

- **Formal vs. Informal:** Tweak your tone depending on the setting. Formal for emails to professors, casual for your friends—save the seriousness for when it's actually needed!

- **Conflict Resolution:** When it comes to conflicts, keep it calm. Use the sandwich approach—start with something nice, address the issue, then finish with another positive note. Everyone leaves happy, and you get bonus points for diplomacy!

- **Feedback Delivery:** When giving feedback, be constructive. Mention something positive first, then talk about what can be improved. It's like topping off your coffee with a dollop of cream—makes it way easier to digest!

Savoring the Perfect Brew

The Filter Coffee Technique is a blend of patience, clarity, empathy, consistency, and adaptability. By applying these principles, you can make your communication as satisfying and effective as a cup of freshly brewed filter coffee. Remember, good communication is an art—it takes practice and a sprinkle of humor. So, brew your words with care, savor those interactions, and watch your life become richer and more fulfilling (because who doesn't want a side of happiness with their coffee?).

Social Attention Holding Theory:

Ah, social attention holding theory—a mouthful of a name for something we all do without realizing it. Imagine this: you're at a college party, trying to impress that cute senior from your department. You've rehearsed your introduction a dozen times in your head, making sure you come off as charming, not clumsy. What you're essentially doing is playing by the rules of social attention holding theory.

In simple terms, it's the idea that in social interactions, we try to capture and maintain the attention of others. It's like being on stage, performing in a play where the audience's interest is your applause meter.

Picture yourself in the midst of a heated debate during a class discussion on Indian politics. You're not just arguing points; you're trying to keep everyone glued to your arguments like a Bollywood blockbuster.

The Art of Attention Holding

Ever feel like your attention span is shorter than that of a goldfish? You're definitely not alone. In our hyperconnected world, grabbing and keeping someone's attention is like trying to eat pani puri without spilling—tricky and messy, but incredibly satisfying once you nail it. Welcome to the art of holding attention, where we'll explore the secrets of keeping your audience engaged from start to finish.

In today's world, instant gratification isn' just a trend; it's practically a way of life. Imagine this: you've got a mountain of assignments to tackle, deadlines looming like thunderclouds, and what do you find yourself doing? Binge-watching that new series that just dropped on your favorite streaming platform, of course! Because, hey, who can resist the allure of drama-packed episodes just a click away when you're drowning in study notes?

It's not just about entertainment either. Take online shopping, for instance. You start with the noble intention of buying that one textbook you desperately need for your upcoming exam. But two hours and a dozen unnecessary purchases later (including a pair of new Nike sneakers because, hey, it was on sale), you realize your original goal got buried under a pile of impulse buys.

And don't even get me started on social media. You innocently log in to check notifications, and before you know it, you've fallen into the deep abyss of memes, cat videos, and endless scrolling. You tell yourself it's just a five-minute break, but an hour later, you're knee-deep in a heated debate about which places sells the best vada pav with someone you've never even met.

Information Overload - The Paradox of Choice

The sheer volume of information available at our fingertips is staggering. From news articles to social media updates, emails to advertisements, we are bombarded with more content than our brains can process. This constant influx creates a competition for our limited attention span, making it difficult for any single piece of information to stand out. A Recent statistic estimated that the average person is exposed to between 6,000 to 10,000 ads every single day.

With so much information vying for our attention, our brains have to work harder to filter out what's irrelevant and focus on what's important, leading to cognitive fatigue and decreased attention spans.

With so many options available for entertainment, education, and information, we often find ourselves overwhelmed by choice. This paradox of choice can lead to decision fatigue, where the effort of choosing what to focus on becomes exhausting. As a result, we may end up skimming through content without truly engaging with it, always on the lookout for something better or more interesting just a click away.

The dark arts of holding attention

Yes, I can state the same old tactics and formulas that you will find on every other website or blog about how to hold the attention of your audience or how to engage people in a conversation. Like Be confident, use body language, engage the audience by asking questions. But we aren't here to state the obvious. The whole idea of this book was to talk about thing that aren't being talked about much so let me introduce you to the Dark arts of How to Hold attention. The technique specially curated by me to give you an edge over all the commoners out there. The stuff no one talks about.

Gamification

In its most basic sense gamification involves applying game mechanics to non-game environments, The goal is to enhance interaction, encourage desired behaviors, and foster a sense of engagement.

The Psychological Basis of Gamification

The success of gamification is rooted in several psychological principles:

- **Intrinsic Motivation**: People are motivated by internal rewards such as personal growth, mastery.

- **Extrinsic Motivation**: External rewards like points, badges, and leaderboards can drive behavior.

- **Social Interaction**: Humans are social creatures who seek interaction, competition, and recognition from peers.

- **Progression and Feedback**: Clear goals and immediate feedback help individuals understand their progress and stay motivated.

Now you would be thinking wait isn't gamification generally used in business, education and workplace environment, yes you are absolutely right it is. It is used to give incentives, track performance and growth and motivate people in such environment.

Here comes the part where we apply gamification for the very first time to the art of holing attention.

In a workplace, intrinsic and extrinsic motivators push employees to work hard and reach the goals set by senior management.

Similarly, in conversations or speeches, you need to make your audience, or counterparts feel like they're playing a game—one where their behaviors or responses earn them your attention and interaction. Yes, I know how that sounds, but hear me out.

In today's world, where people consume millions of bits of information every minute, the only way to truly hold someone's attention is by making them work for it. When they're actively vying for your attention, that's when they're fully engaged. Now, imagine turning this into a game. Create "levels" in your interactions—each level they reach rewards them with more of your attention and engagement. It's like giving them a place in your consciousness, where they have to earn the privilege of being truly noticed by you.

The Concept of Levels

Level 1: Demand Attention

Description: At this initial level, interaction is minimal. It involves setting yourself in a position where you demand the attention of others, you have to make sure you are in the position where you have authority or control over the conversation that is about to begin.

Be confident Be Controversial Demand Attention.

Once you kick off a conversation, make sure to keep it lively and centered around you. Share your stories or opinions in a way that gets people curious and prompts them to ask questions or chime in with their own thoughts. Don't shy away from bringing up controversial topics; in fact, they're like conversation magnets. They push people to engage, debate, or passionately agree, making the chat more dynamic and memorable. Not only that but, they can also create a sense of intimacy and attraction. There's something about diving into a hot topic that can bring people closer, making the conversation feel more personal and engaging.

It's like planting a little flag in their brains with your unique take on things, and who knows, it might even spark some friendly arguments! Your aim is to be the person everyone is eager to listen to.

Here your interaction with your audience or counterparts is just acknowledging them nothing more than that.

Reward: Basic acknowledgment and Eye contact

Level 2: Engaged Interaction

Description:

Talk about yourself—yes, I know this might seem to go against the core principles from one of my favorite books, *How to Win Friends and Influence People*, where showing interest in others and listening more is key. But, let's be honest—this is the dark arts we're discussing here. So yes, talk about yourself to intrigue others.

Of course, you can't just keep praising yourself or spouting random facts. The trick is to be subtle and manipulative with your words. The goal is to create genuine interest in you, to make people want to engage in conversation, observe your body language, and subconsciously gravitate toward you. At the very least, they should feel compelled to interact. Mastering this gives you a certain power over others, making you the one they're paying attention to.

You Are the Centre: Handle Distractions with Grace

Now that you've successfully captured and engaged your audience's attention, the challenge shifts to maintaining that focus. Being the center of attention isn't just about speaking well or having interesting things to say—it's also about how you handle the inevitable distractions that arise in any social situation. This is the tough part, where many falter, but with the right approach, you can keep the spotlight firmly on you.

Strategies to Maintain Attention:

- **Stay Composed:** Distractions are a natural part of any conversation. Whether it's someone interrupting, an off-topic comment, or external noise, your ability to remain composed is crucial. Don't let distractions rattle you or pull you off course. Instead, acknowledge them calmly, and then smoothly steer the conversation back to your main points.

- **Integrate the Distraction:** Sometimes, the best way to handle a distraction is to integrate it into the conversation. If someone brings up an off-topic point, use it as a springboard to return to your narrative. For example, if a new topic is introduced, find a way to link it back to what you were saying. This not only shows that you're in control but also that you're adaptable and quick-witted.

- **Use Humor:** Humor is a powerful tool in managing distractions. A well-placed joke or light-hearted comment can diffuse tension and recapture everyone's attention. It shows that you're not easily flustered and can turn potential disruptions into moments that reinforce your role as the conversation leader.

- **Redirect Focus:** If someone else tries to take control of the conversation or if the group's attention starts to drift, gently redirect the focus back to you. You can do this by posing a thought-provoking question, introducing a new and interesting topic, or even by directly addressing someone in the group, drawing their attention back to the main conversation.

- **Stay Engaging:** Continuously keep the conversation lively and engaging by introducing new elements or asking for opinions. This prevents others from getting bored or distracted in the first place. The more captivating you are, the less likely people are to lose focus.

Level 3: Active Participation
Description:

you've gone beyond just grabbing attention—now, you're focused on making your personal conversations and interactions within your social circle more meaningful and collaborative. This stage is about encouraging others to actively engage with you, whether in one-on-one conversations, group discussions with friends, or while trying to impress someone special. Your aim is to foster deeper connections and mutual investment in the dialogue.

Strategies to Encourage Active Participation:

1. Share Personal Stories: By sharing something personal or meaningful about yourself, you invite others to do the same. When you reveal your thoughts, experiences, or feelings, it creates a sense of intimacy and encourages the other person to participate more actively by sharing their own stories.

2. Show Genuine Interest: Make it clear that you're truly interested in what others have to say. Use active listening techniques, like nodding, maintaining eye contact, and asking follow-up questions. This not only keeps the conversation flowing but also makes the other person feel valued and understood.

3. Create Shared Experiences: Suggest activities or discussions that everyone can contribute to, like planning a group outing or debating a fun, controversial topic. These shared experiences help bond the group and make everyone feel included.

4. Balance Talking and Listening: While it's important to share your thoughts and experiences, it's equally crucial to give others space to speak. In conversations where you're trying to impress someone, listening more than you talk can actually leave a stronger impression, as it shows that you value their perspective.

Rewards:

Be more readily available and provide space for more connected conversation.

Allow others to initiate conversations with yourself.

Level 4: Inner Circle

Description:

At this highest level, the dynamics shift from basic interaction to deep personal connection. The individuals who reach this stage have proven their worth and loyalty over time. They're not just acquaintances but trusted friends or confidants who hold a special place in your life. Engaging with them involves a level of intimacy and openness that goes beyond casual conversation. This stage is about creating lasting bonds and sharing deeper aspects of yourself.

Strategies to Foster an Inner Circle:

Share Vulnerabilities:

Open up about your personal struggles, dreams, and insecurities. By sharing these intimate details, you create a safe space for them to do the same. This mutual exchange of vulnerabilities builds trust and strengthens your bond.

Be Reliable and Supportive:

Consistently show that you're there for them, whether it's celebrating their successes or offering support during tough times. Reliability is crucial in maintaining close relationships and ensures that they feel valued and supported.

Encourage Deep Conversations:

Engage in discussions that go beyond surface-level topics. Talk about your values, beliefs, and long-term goals. These deeper conversations help forge a stronger connection and show that you value their perspective and input.

Respect Boundaries:

Even within your inner circle, it is important to respect personal boundaries. Understand their comfort zones and avoid pushing them into uncomfortable situations. Mutual respect is key to maintaining a healthy, long-lasting relationship.

Rewards:

By being part of someone's inner circle, you enjoy the perks of constant communication, always staying connected. Reward them by develop a deep personal bond where their thoughts and emotions are met with genuine care and understanding. Provide them elevated status within your social circles, become someone others look for advice and support. This not only proves to other that you are a reliable and trusted individual, but you gain a certain over of others that makes them trust you with their decisions and loyalty. Congrats once you successfully reached level 4 you have created a place for yourself in their subconscious you have achieved exactly what you set out to achieve holing their undivided attention.

The Power of Priming: A Deep Dive into an Influential Psychological

Priming is a psychological phenomenon where exposure to one stimulus influences how a person responds to a subsequent stimulus, often without conscious awareness. It's a powerful tool that can subtly shape perceptions, attitudes, and behaviors, making it highly effective in both personal and social interactions. Understanding and using priming can help you capture and hold attention, steer conversations, and create more impactful experiences. Understanding Priming works by activating certain associations in memory just before carrying out an action or task. These associations influence how we perceive, think, and behave in subsequent situations. For example, if someone is primed with the word "warm," they might be more likely to describe a person as friendly or kind compared to someone primed with the word "cold." Priming can occur in various forms: -

Semantic Priming: This involves words or concepts that are related in meaning. For example, the word "doctor" might prime someone to think of the word "nurse" more quickly than they would think of an unrelated word like "butter." -

Perceptual Priming: This involves stimuli that are visually or audibly similar. Seeing a picture of a tree might make you more likely to recognize the word "forest" later on. -

Associative Priming: This involves related ideas that are connected through experience. For instance, hearing a particular song might prime you to think of a specific event or time period in your life.

Subliminal Priming: involves stimuli that are presented so quickly or subtly that they are not consciously perceived. - Example: A quick flash of a smiling face in a video might make the audience feel more positive, even if they don't consciously notice it.

Positive priming : involves using stimuli that evoke positive emotions before important interactions. This can make people more receptive and attentive to what you have to say. - Example: share a positive story, compliment, or engaging visual. This creates a positive atmosphere, making others more likely to engage with you favorably.

How Priming Works Priming operates through a few key mechanisms: -

Activation of Mental Representations: When you are exposed to a stimulus, it activates a network of related concepts in your mind. These concepts become more accessible and can influence your thoughts, feelings, and actions.

Subconscious Influence: Priming often occurs below the level of conscious awareness. You might not realize that a previous stimulus is affecting your current behavior, making it a subtle yet powerful tool. -

Temporal Proximity: The effects of priming are usually strongest when the priming stimulus and the target action or response occur close together in time.

Priming is a secret weapon in the art of holding attention, winning in social situations, and subtly influencing your surroundings to get what you want—all while making it seem like you're just a charming conversationalist. It's like having a cheat code for social dynamics, helping you stay one step ahead, whether you're steering a conversation or making a lasting impression. Here's how priming can work its magic in real-life scenarios:

Capturing and Holding Attention

Imagine walking into a room and needing to command the crowd's attention. You don't want to scream, "Hey, listen to me!"—that's too obvious and, frankly, a bit desperate. Instead, you drop subtle hints that grab people's focus without them even realizing it. Start with positive priming: share an uplifting anecdote or compliment the setting. This warms up the room, activating positive emotions and making people more attentive. You've now primed them to associate you with good vibes, and—voilà—you've hooked their attention before you even dive into your main point.

Winning in Social Situations

Ever wonder why some people seem to glide through social gatherings with ease, effortlessly building connections? Chances are, they're using some form of priming, whether they know it or not. Before diving into deeper topics, they might casually mention something relatable—a shared experience, a mutual acquaintance, or even a popular show that everyone's binge-watching. By priming their audience with these familiar topics, they lay the groundwork for rapport. People start nodding along, feeling that sense of connection, and boom—you're the life of the party without breaking a sweat. Even in more competitive settings, like negotiating or selling an idea, priming works wonders. Just subtly introduce concepts or images that align with your goal (think about mentioning success stories or showing visuals of achievement), and you've got people primed to agree with you before they realize what's happening.

Manipulating Surroundings to Get What You Want

Let's face it—sometimes, getting what you want involves a bit of strategic manipulation (in the nicest way possible, of course!). Priming is your low-key way to influence outcomes without appearing pushy. Got a presentation or a project you want the prof to love? Before your big moment, subtly drop references to topics they're obsessed with. "Oh, sir, I read this article on renewable energy, just like you mentioned in the last lecture..." Now they're primed, mentally tuned into your wavelength, and by the time you present, they're already nodding along. You might as well prepare for that "A" grade! you've just primed their brain to be more receptive to your proposal. They won't know why they're nodding in agreement, but you will.

Priming isn't just about being clever—it's about reading the room and planting the right mental seeds. It is a subtle, powerful way to guide conversations, shape perceptions, and—let's be honest—get what you want, all while keeping a smile on your face and everyone else none the wiser. So go ahead, prime away—you've got this social game on lock.

The Theory of Planned Behavior (TPB) by Icek Ajzen

is like a cheat sheet for understanding why we humans do what we do. It says our actions are mainly driven by three things:

1. **Attitudes Toward the Behavior**
2. **Subjective Norms**
3. **Perceived Behavioral Control**

These factors combine to shape our intentions, which in turn predict what we'll actually end up doing. Think of it like a roadmap for all those times we make big decisions, like choosing between preparing for an exam or binge-watching the latest series.

Attitudes Toward the Behavior

Attitudes represent how positively or negatively an individual perceives the behavior. Attitudes depend on two things:

- **Behavioral Beliefs**: What do you *believe* will happen if you actually do the thing? For instance, if you think studying will get you a good job, you're more likely to hit the books. But if you think nothing can save you maybe not so much.

- **Outcome Evaluation**: How much do you *value* those outcomes? If your dream is to land a great job, studying seems like a worthy investment. If your dream is to become an *influencer* well, that might be another story.

Subjective Norms

This is basically log kya kahenge (what will people say), but with a psychological twist. It's all about the social pressure you feel—whether it's from your parents, friends, or even your professor. Do they expect you to show up to class? To score well? To hit the gym and stop ordering biryani every other day?

- **Normative Beliefs:** These are your thoughts about what the important people in your life think you should be doing. If your friends are all pulling all-nighters before the exam, you'll probably feel the pressure to do the same. Or at least pretend you are.

- **Motivation to Comply:** Now, this is where it gets fun. Just because someone expects something from you doesn't mean you'll actually listen. It depends on how much you care about their opinion. If your bestie says, "Let's go for a walk instead of that third cup of chai," you might comply. But if it's your mom telling you to study when you've already committed to Netflix—well, you know how that goes.

3. Perceived Behavioral Control

This is all about how confident you feel in your ability to actually *do* the thing. If you think you can pull off studying for three hours straight, or stick to that new workout plan, you're more likely to follow through. On the other hand, if you're already doubting yourself (looking at you, procrastinators), the odds aren't in your favor.

- **Control Beliefs:** These are your thoughts about what could help or stop you from doing the behavior. Think of them as the pros and cons of actually pulling it off. Did your WIFI suddenly stop working when you *finally* sat down to study? Is your gym too far and Zomato too convenient? All these little things add up.

- **Perceived Power:** This is about how much you think those factors are in or out of your control. If you believe you can work around the distractions, like studying at the library or hiding your phone, you've got a better shot at succeeding.

Intentions and Behavior

- **Behavioral Intentions:** This is the part where you *intend* to do something, which, let's face it, doesn't always mean you actually will. You might have full intentions to study for tomorrow's test, but somehow, after scrolling through one too many memes, your plan goes sideways. The stronger your intention, the more likely you are to follow through. That's the theory, at least.

- **Actual Behavior:** Finally, the big one—whether or not you actually do the thing! While intentions are usually a good predictor, life has a way of throwing you off track. Maybe you planned to study all night, but your friends pulled you into a chai break that turned into a full-blown hangout. Hey, it happens!